Making Music Your Business

Making Music Your Business

A Practical Guide to Making $ Doing What You Love

by Traci Truly
Attorney at Law

SPHINX® PUBLISHING
AN IMPRINT OF SOURCEBOOKS, INC.®
NAPERVILLE, ILLINOIS
www.SphinxLegal.com

First Edition: 2005

Published by: **Sphinx® Publishing, An Imprint of Sourcebooks, Inc.®**

Naperville Office
P.O. Box 4410
Naperville, Illinois 60567-4410
630-961-3900
Fax: 630-961-2168
www.sourcebooks.com
www.SphinxLegal.com

This publication is designed to provide accurate and authoritative information in regard
to the subject matter covered. It is sold with the understanding that the publisher is not
engaged in rendering legal, accounting, or other professional service. If legal advice or
other expert assistance is required, the services of a competent professional person
should be sought.
From a Declaration of Principles Jointly Adopted by a Committee of the
American Bar Association and a Committee of Publishers and Associations

This product is not a substitute for legal advice.
Disclaimer required by Texas statutes.

Library of Congress Cataloging-in-Publication Data
Truly, Traci.
  Making music your business : a practical guide to making $ doing what you
love /
by Traci Truly.-- 1st ed.
    p. cm.
  Includes index.
  ISBN 1-57248-486-1 (pbk. : alk. paper)
  1. Music--Vocational guidance--United States. 2. Music trade--Vocational
guidance--United States. I. Title.

ML3795.T78 2005
780'.23'73--dc22
                                                                    2005011563

Printed and bound in the United States of America.
                        BG — 10 9 8 7 6 5 4 3 2 1

For my mother, Bette Truly.

Acknowledgments

Thanks to Don Brooks of *Omni Entertainment, Inc.* and *Caprice Records* and to *Mustang Booking Agency* (all of Dallas) for the practical information from the industry side.

Thanks to Bette Truly for patiently reading each of my manuscripts.

Contents

Introduction

Music captures the imaginations of millions of people. While most of us are content to listen to the radio and buy CDs, there are still thousands of others who want to make music their life's work. It's a tough business, and professional musicians face many challenges, but it also offers the opportunity for significant rewards. Every year, a new artist or band reaches the highest levels of recognition and financial compensation. Many more remain as regional or local artists. No matter what your present level, the more you know about the business, the better your odds of achieving your goals.

No matter how small you are right now, you will find tips and strategies in this book to help you present yourself as a professional musician. The more professional your image, the more opportunities you will get to reach the next level. You can use the information in this book on each step of the way.

As you are just starting your career, handling yourself in as a professional makes you seem bigger than you are. This will help your career locally and will definitely help as you begin trying to get shows outside your home area.

The first section deals with the basic business aspects of your musical career. The basics of starting and running a business are discussed, including how to structure your band and how to deal with issues related to your stage name. Following that is a discussion on the various professionals you will encounter—managers, business managers, talent or booking agents, and attorneys. You will find a section on the business aspects of performing and touring, as well as chapters on dealing with record labels and on promoting your band and your material. Because there are always legal issues related to any business, many of those are covered too. There are chapters on copyright and trademark issues and on music publishing (which is the process of licensing your music for others to use).

A few sample forms are also included. When looking at them, please remember that laws vary from state to state (and from country to country), and these forms are not, and cannot be, designed to be accurate for all states and countries. They are here only to give you the basic idea. You should always check out the laws of the state in which you are doing business.

chapter one:
The Business of the Band

As a musician, your primary focus has probably been perfecting your musical skills and writing original material. However, if you plan on making music your career, or even if you just want to play a gig here and there, you must recognize that the music business is just that—a *business*. Because it can be a difficult and harsh business, the more you know about how the industry works, the better off you will be.

You should also recognize that you need to approach your music career as a business. This means that starting a band should be similar to starting any other kind of business. Although there are some different issues involved, the same is true if you are a solo artist and not part of a band. Therefore, the first issues you need to address are those involved in starting a new business.

FORMING YOUR NEW BUSINESS

Your first step is to choose the *form* of your business. For a group of musicians, the two basic choices are a *partnership* or a *corporation*. If you are a solo artist, you also have the option of operating as a *sole proprietorship*. It will be up to you to choose one of these options in the beginning of your career. However, as you progress and sign a management agreement, your management company may have contractual requirements that govern which form of business you use.

Each form offers different advantages and protections, and each has different limitations. Cost concerns may initially play a role in choosing your form of business. You should consider consulting with an accountant and an attorney to help you with this decision. Learn as much as you can about the differences between all the forms so that you can make the best choice for your situation. It is always easier to do something right from the beginning, than it is to go in later and try to straighten it out. The same is true for getting the structure of your business in place at the beginning of your career.

PARTNERSHIPS

By default, most new bands operate as *partnerships*, even though the group members may not even realize this is the case. When two or more people operate a business without formal business documents, they are operating as a partnership. There are tax and liability considerations involved, even if your band does not have formal partnership agreements in place. Given these facts, any band would be well served to minimally have a *written partnership agreement*. The band should consider consulting an attorney to obtain advice about what is involved in doing business as a partnership, and perhaps even hire the attorney to draft formal partnership documents.

One of the most important issues that your band needs to address in the partnership agreement is the ownership of material written by members of the band. If more than one member of the group collaborates on a song, the band must have an agreement in place to determine what percentage is owned by each member. It is much easier to determine these issues as each song is written than it will be once there is money on the table.

Having an agreement in place will help answer a variety of questions.

- What happens when a member leaves the band, either voluntarily or because the other members have asked the member to leave the band?
- If that person has written songs or parts of songs, does the band still have the right to exploit these songs?
- Does the departing member have to be paid a fee for the band to play the song?
- What happens to CDs or other recordings on which the departing member has played?
- What if the band gets a record deal after the member leaves?
- Can the band use the songs written by the former member?
- If they use a song written by the former member, will he or she be entitled to compensation?

Getting an agreement on these issues will not be easy once the band member is gone, particularly if the band member has been asked to leave the band. Having a partnership agreement done is advance, when everyone is still on friendly terms, helps to lessen these kinds of difficulties. Creating a doc-

Musical Note

A critical issue is the *ownership of* and *rights to* the use of the band's name. Issues related to the band's name are discussed in more detail in Chapter 2.

ument that answers some of the questions a band can face down the road takes only a few minutes at a band practice, and saves a lot of time that would otherwise be lost to fighting later. It can also serve as the guideline when the band is ready to register its material with a performing rights society, obtain a copyright, or license its material for commercial use. If the agreement is reached at the time the song is written, there is less opportunity for disagreement between the band members on the respective contributions of each member later on. As the band becomes more advanced, you can skip this step and go directly to formally registering the material at the time it is created. (Registering and performance rights organizations are discussed in Chapter 8.)

Tax Issues

When your band plays gigs for money, the band may be required to file a tax return. If there is more than one member of the band, you will be treated as a partnership for income tax purposes. This is true even if you do not have a formal partnership agreement.

When the band is paid by the venues, the venues will ask for a tax identification number. If the band has not formally created a partnership and obtained a federal tax identification number, one of the band members will have to give the club his or her Social Security number. That income will then be reported to the Internal Revenue Service as personal income to that band member. This creates a problem for the band member whose Social Security number is used, and potentially creates tax-related problems for all members of the band if all the tax reporting problems are not properly addressed.

For those of you who live in states with personal income tax, you can also end up with problems with your state tax authorities. Most states also have business taxes that must be paid. If you do not know what the rules in your state are, you can find yourself with tax problems that require expensive professional help to resolve. You may also find yourself paying fines and penalties that can be avoided with the proper advance planning.

In order to avoid these problems, you should formally create your partnership and obtain a tax identification number for it. You can then provide this number to venues for tax reporting purposes and also open a bank account in the partnership name.

One significant problem with doing business as a partnership is the liability issue. In a partnership, the personal assets of each partner are liable for the acts of any of the partners. This means that if one of the band members injures someone while driving the band's trailer to a show, each band member could be required to pay all of the damages out of his or her personal property. If a member gets credit in the partnership name and defaults, then the other individual members can be forced to pay. In some states, that may mean if you own a house, your house could be taken to pay that debt.

Self-Employment Tax

As a musician, you may run into situations in which a venue or a band wants to hire you for a single show or recording. In that event, you will not be a full-time employee for that business, but may just be *contract labor* or working *for hire*. If that happens, the person hiring you will not be holding out any taxes from your check, and you will have to be responsible for paying all the taxes yourself. It counts as *self-employment income* in this situation, so you must remember that you have to pay your federal income taxes and all of the Social Security tax (as opposed to half when you are an employee and your employer pays the other half). You must keep good records of the money you make under these circumstances, because you are essentially in business for yourself.

CORPORATIONS

The best way to avoid that liability problem is to do business as a *corporation*. A corporation is a separate legal entity and has the significant advantage of providing a shield to protect the personal assets of the owners of the corporation from the liabilities and debts of the corporation. Another advantage to a corporation is that its duration is *perpetual*. In a partnership, if one partner leaves, the partnership is dissolved and a new one is created between the remaining partners and any new band members. With a corporation, this is no longer an issue. As band members come and go, the legal entity of the corporation is not affected.

One disadvantage to a corporation is that it does cost money to form. Although the amount charged by each state varies, there will be some sort of fee due to the state in which you incorporate. You may also have to pay fees to a professional—such as an attorney—to prepare the documents needed. However, there are other sources for help in creating a corporation. There are books available that will help if you decide to do the corporation paperwork on your own.

There are two main types of corporations—*S corporations* and *C corporations*. They both offer liability protection, but each has different treatment under the tax laws. You should get advice from a tax professional as to which type of corporation your band should become.

In addition to the traditional corporations, there is an entity called a *limited liability company*. It is set up similarly to corporations and has the same liability protection, but has some tax treatment options that are different from those available to the regular corporation. Once again, you should consult with a tax professional for help in making this decision.

Because a corporation is a separate legal entity, it will have to file state and federal tax returns. The corporation will also have to withhold taxes from the salaries paid to any corporate employees and provide the employees with a *W-2*. This can be an advantage for the band members because it simplifies their individual tax returns, but does require some additional paperwork. Because the corporation will have employees (at a minimum, the band members themselves), the corporation will also have to file reports and pay unemployment compensation taxes in most states. Having a corporation also means maintaining corporate records, holding annual meetings of the board of directors and the shareholders, and keeping records of these meetings. Obviously, there is additional expense and time involved in meeting these requirements.

An artist who is not serious about music as a career may not wish to undertake these obligations. However, a musician who plans to have a career in the music industry will find that, at some point, they will need to incorporate. There are clear advantages to getting this done early in your career, so that your procedures and paperwork are in place and operational from the beginning. While forming a corporation does require some costs at the beginning and a little more work on your part to form it and keep up with the extra tax and reporting obligations, as a general rule the benefits to having the protection of a corporation outweigh the costs and the effort involved.

Corporate Name

When you incorporate your band, you will have to select a name for the corporation. The name can be the same as your band name or it can be another name. The state in which you incorporate will have to approve the name you choose as your corporate name. Every state requires that every official corporate name registered in that state be unique. If your name is the same as or very close to the name of another existing corporation, you will have to pick a different name.

If you incorporate under a name other than the name of the band, you will also have to file an *assumed name* to show that the corporation owns the name of the band. Generally, the assumed name certificates are filed in the county in which the business is located (your band's home county), as well as with the state corporations department.

Additional Documents

As part of the incorporation documents, you will need *bylaws*. This document contains the terms and conditions under which the corporate business will be conducted. Since it will probably be agreed that each band member will be a shareholder in the corporation, you should also create a shareholders' agreement that sets out the terms for buying out the shares of corporate stock from a band member who either quits the band, is fired, dies, or becomes disabled. (Sample forms for Articles of Incorporation and Bylaws for a Texas corporation are included in the appendix. You will need to check the laws of your state for the

Musical Note

Since one person can incorporate a business, the corporate structure is available for solo artists as well as for groups.

appropriate form, and Texas residents will need to check for changes in the law.)

GENERAL BUSINESS PROVISIONS

Once the band is incorporated or the partnership formed, the next step is for the business to obtain a tax identification number and open a bank account. Your tax identification number can be obtained by calling the Internal Revenue Service at 800-829-4933 or by mailing in IRS Form *SS-4*. This form is available online from the IRS website at **www.irs.gov**.

From this point forward, all band funds should be paid into the business bank account. All band expenses should be paid out of the business account. It is important to keep all your receipts, as well as any other documentation you get related to band income and expenses. You will need this information to file the corporate or partnership tax returns. The individual members must remember that any time they take money out of the corporate account for their personal use, it is considered income to them and must be reported on a *W-2* at the end of each year. It is also important to remember that any equipment bought with funds taken from the corporate account belong to the corporation and not to the individual band member using the equipment.

The same thing is true if you are operating as a partnership. Any money that you take personally is treated for tax purposes as a distribution of partnership profits and is taxable income to the band member. Any time you take money for your personal use that has been earned from your music career, you should keep records of it. If you are a corporation, monies should always be paid to the band members from the corporate bank account, and you should not just take cash from a show and keep it.

Additionally, each employee of the corporation or partnership needs to sign an employment agreement with the corporation or partnership. This applies to band members and any other employees, such as road crew members. The band member's contract should address issues such as compensation and ownership of music created while the individual works for the corporation or partnership or license rights to use recordings created during the employment period. Other important issues include the length of the contract term, the perks that will be included, the grounds for termination of the employment contract, vacation terms, and the provisions that apply in the event of death or disability of the band member. Employment contracts should also include a listing of the duties to be undertaken by the employee. You may also want to consider confidentiality provisions in the agreement so that a departing employee does not take confidential information or material with them when they leave. Social Security numbers for each employee should always be obtained.

 Musical Note

Most states will have provisions that require businesses to notify the state of new employees that have been hired. You can use the W-4 form you used to get the employee's Social Security number for this. Each state has a specific office in which this form must be filed.

If any of your band members or band employees are not U.S. citizens, the band must ensure that they have proper immigration documents and work permits. Failure to take these steps can result in significant fines and penalties. Therefore, you should require each employee to complete an *Employment Verification Form* (Form I-9). If your band has a member or employee that is not a

U.S. citizen, you should consult with an attorney for advice on this issue.

Also note that your band, like any other business, is subject to all of the anti-discrimination, sexual harassment, and other labor laws. Included among these laws are the child labor laws, which can become a factor if any of the band members is under the age of 18. These laws vary from state to state, but generally restrict the amount of time a minor can spend working. The ages at which these laws apply also vary from state to state.

Another note to remember about minors is that they lack the legal ability to sign contracts or own and manage property. That means that if any band members are under age 18, they should not own shares of stock in the corporation in their own names, and they cannot legally manage partnership or corporate business affairs. If your band is in this situation, you should consult an attorney to help your band determine how to best handle this situation. Some states may allow a parent or guardian to sign the contract for the minor. In addition, some states have provisions that require entertainment contracts for underage artists be approved by a judge. You will need the assistance of an attorney to complete these procedures.

Insurance

Another important aspect of your business that must be considered is the need for insurance. Any time your band owns transportation equipment, it must be insured before it is driven. Worker's compensation insurance, which protects your business if someone gets hurt while they are working for you, and unemployment insurance becomes mandatory when you reach a certain number of employees. Even if workers' compensation insurance is not mandatory, you may want to consider buying it anyway. If you have it, and someone gets hurt while they are working for you (for example, one of your crew members hurts his back setting up your equipment for a show), the insurance company pays his medical bills and lost wages. Without it, the band can be required to pay these things, and this can be very expensive.

When you can afford it, there are other types of insurance that are important in helping protect and preserve the assets of the band. Liability insurance can provide coverage if your equipment is damaged and if a company employee injures someone while on the job. At some point, your company can also get a group health insurance policy for the members of the band and any other employees.

chapter two:
The Business of the Band's Name

Selecting the name under which an artist performs is a critical early step. There are many issues to be considered as this decision is made. Some of the issues are clear—you need to select a name that is appropriate for your genre of music and that you can use effectively as a marketing tool. If you plan on a career in music, and hope to get commercial airplay for your band, you need to keep in mind that there are restrictions imposed by the *Federal Communications Commission* as to what words can be said on radio and television. A name that violates these restrictions may not be the best long-term choice for your band, even if everyone in the club scene thinks the name you have chosen is clever or funny.

It should be obvious that you cannot use the same name as other bands. *The Rolling Stones* is a great name for a band, but it is definitely not available for your band to use. If you start out using the same name as another established band, you can expect to receive a letter from their attorney telling you that your band must change its name or you will be sued.

If you have picked a name and are fairly certain that there are not any famous bands using that name, you still cannot safely adopt this name without doing a little research. There may be another small, local band out there using that name already. Rather than run into a conflict about the name down the line, it is always best to do further investigation about name availability before you begin performing and using the name.

CHECKING ON NAME AVAILABILITY

First, you should check to see if your preferred name has been *service marked* by someone else. As a general rule, you will hear the terms *trademark* and *service mark* used interchangeably, but technically the band name is a service mark. A service mark is any word, name, symbol, or device used in commerce to identify and distinguish the services of one provider from that of another. A trademark applies to a product, so you will actually be searching for service marks.

You can do this search yourself or you can obtain professional assistance. To search yourself, begin with the U.S. Patent and Trademark Office. The most efficient way to access these records is through its website at **www.uspto.gov**. To search for name availability, click the "How to Search" button and follow the instructions. For professional assistance, you can either hire an attorney or a search service. There are many search services listed online. Find them by entering the phrase "trademark searches" in any search engine.

You should also run an Internet search on the name. In addition to just putting the name into a search engine, you will also want to check Web address availability for your band's name. It is important to have a Web address that uses your band's name so that your fans can easily find your website. Once you have used one or more of the search engines and you find that the name is available, go to one of the sites that offer domain name registration and reserve your name.

Special Concerns for the Solo Artist

You may think that if you are a solo artist planning to perform under your given name, none of these issues apply to you. However, this is not the case. You need to follow all of the steps outlined above to protect your right to use your name as your stage name and to ensure that you do not waste time establishing yourself under one name only to have to change it later. This is particularly important if you have a fairly common name.

chapter three:
Managers and Management Companies

At some point in your musical career, you will confront the decision of whether or not to hire a management company. A manager can either be your band's best tool for success or its worst nightmare. Which company to hire should be carefully considered, because you and your management company need to have the same goals in mind for your band. It is also important for you and your manager to be on the same page when it comes to how those goals will be achieved. In a good manager/band situation, you and your manager will be working closely together on a regular basis, especially early in your musical career. An otherwise good relationship can be ruined if each of you does not understand and agree with the expectations of the other, or if you have radically different ideas about how your goals will be achieved.

WHAT A MANAGER DOES

At the most basic level, a manager is an advisor. Managers give advice about all areas of your music career. As a new band starting out, a manager can help you develop a marketable image and an effective stage presence. New bands often need help determining what material, and how much of it, should be included on a CD. Managers can also be an important asset when it comes to evaluating the quality of your recordings. If you have an inferior CD, your manager can help you get to a good producer and get a good quality recording. Once this is in place, your manager can help further your career by shopping your recording to record labels to help you get a record deal, working to find other distribution channels for your recordings and merchandise, and trying to get radio airplay for your band.

As you become a more established band, your manager will help you evaluate the opportunities that come your way. Not every offer or opportunity should be accepted. On the other hand, there are shows that the band may not want to play that would be good for the band. A good manager can help you to know the difference.

A manager is an important part of your team when it comes time to try for a record deal, especially when you are dealing with a major label, mini-major label, or larger, established independent label. The economics of the recording industry have changed a great deal in recent years, and the labels generally want you to already have some songs on a market quality CD. Your manager should be able to provide you with important and helpful advice in this area. Additionally, most labels will not talk to a band without representation of some kind, whether it be a manager or an attorney. (The role attorneys play is discussed in Chapter 6.)

A well-established management company should also be able to open doors for you to help get your material commercial exposure. Your manager can help you know what to put in your press kit—a very important part of marketing your band—and can also help you get that press kit to people who are in a position to further your band's music career.

Managers also help you define your image, which includes things like your stage show and presence, your website, flyers, and posters. The bottom line on the manager's job is that he or she should handle the time-consuming details of getting the band established as a business and should work with the other professionals on your team so that you are free to write, practice, perform, and promote.

Finding a Manager

As a young band just starting out, your choices of management companies will be much more limited than those of a more established band. If you are based in a larger city, there will likely be several local management companies on the scene. Primarily, these companies will be smaller than some of the more famous music management companies.

There are advantages and disadvantages to being represented by a smaller, local management company. On the plus side, a local manager should have good relationships with the local venues and will be able to help your band get good shows just by virtue of the fact that they have signed your band to a management agreement. They will also be able to see most of your local shows and give you better advice about things like your stage presence and image.

Because your manager will have a local presence, they can also help you market your band and establish a professional reputation on the local scene. As some of you may have already discovered, venues do not always want to pay new bands to play shows. A local manager will have the relationships with the booking agents for the clubs to keep this from happening to your band.

A local manager will also be familiar with the other bands playing regularly in your area. This can help you get on bills that help your band and get shows with other local bands that fit your style of music. Obviously, this will help your band build its local fan base.

A local manager should also know what venues in your geographic region are suited to your music and should be able to help you get some out-of-town shows. However, keep in mind that a manager is not a talent agent or booking agent. It is not part of his or her job to find gigs or do other kinds of booking for you.

Of course, there are some disadvantages to using a small management company. A small company may not have the necessary knowledge and ability to open doors for you on a national level. You also need to be sure you are dealing with a reputable, professional company. As you play shows and spend time on your local music scene, you will run into a lot of people who want to be involved in the music scene and hang out with band members. They may present themselves as "managers" when they do not have any qualifications to actually manage a band. You should also be wary of those who offer to *help you out* without a formal manager relationship.

A real management company will expect you to either sign written management contracts or at least specifically negotiate the terms of the relationship, and will expect you to run your band as a professional musical enterprise. If you are considering a manager who does not require these things, you should investigate further before making an agreement of any sort. You should also inquire with other local bands and any connections you have with the local venues to see what kind of reputation your prospective manager and management company have in the area.

Ask any management company who approaches you for a deal for references to other bands they manage—and then check those references. While another band's dissatisfaction with a manager does not mean anything by itself, you can gain valuable information by knowing why they were unhappy with the company. Did they just have legitimate creative differences or was the manager doing drugs at the band's shows? Managers with a less-than-professional approach can be a problem if you are working with a small, local management company.

Musical Note

Managers are not required to have any special training or certification—anyone can call him- or herself a manager.

Know Who Actually Manages You

If you are dealing with a company as opposed to a single individual, you also want to have a clear understanding of who will actually be doing the day-to-day managing of your band. Ideally, you will be able to negotiate an agreement with your management company that contains at least some guidance on this issue. In many instances, you are brought on board with the management company by a particular person who has become familiar with your music and wants to work with you. Do not just assume that this will be the person who actively manages your band. Find out whether or not that is with whom you will be primarily working.

Also, find out what the company's policies are in regard to assigning and reassigning managers to acts on the company roster. You can ask to have a key person clause inserted in the agreement, saying that a particular person will serve as your primary manager. With this clause, if the management company assigns you to someone else, you can terminate the management agreement. Of course, the larger the management company, the less likely they are to agree to such provisions.

You also want to ask, during the negotiation phase, how many other bands with which your manager will be working. If the person you are expecting to manage your career is also personally responsible for fifty other acts, you need to determine how much time and attention your band will be getting from that manager and how much support staff is available to help ease the burden. There is a limit to how much any one person can accomplish, and you may be better off being a lesser-known manager's most important band than being at the very bottom of a well-known manager's priority list. This is a judgment call you will have to make as you decide which manager or management company is the right fit for you and your career.

However, as a new band, do not get so carried away with your status as "stars" (or future stars) that you decide to only do business with the big, national companies, or decide that your band requires a manager in Los Angeles, Nashville, or New York. You can find disreputable managers with offices in those cities just as easily as you can anywhere else. You must also keep in mind that the larger, established companies do not often take on new, untested bands as clients. If they do take you on, you want to be sure that you are not so far down on their roster that you do not get the help you need for achieving your band's goals.

WHAT A MANAGER DOES NOT DO

One of the most important things to remember about your manager is that this a business relationship, and you should treat it as one. Your manager is not your mother, and he or she will not be assuming responsibility for every part of your life and the life of your band. You and the other members of your band will still have to work to promote your band, and you will have to learn to balance all of the responsibilities in your life.

Unless you are very fortunate, you will need some method of supporting yourself until your career becomes more established. For most of you, this will mean you will have to have a job. You may also have a spouse, significant other, or even children. It can be very difficult to balance these competing demands on your time, and it can be tempting to want to push all of the work of the band onto your manager.

If your band has progressed enough to convince a management company to work with you, you have probably spent a great deal of time practicing and writing new material. You have probably also worked hard to promote your band and build some sort of following. Just because you now have a manager does not mean that you can quit these activities. One of the fastest ways to alienate your new manager, particularly as a new band, is to quit promoting your shows and expect the management company to do everything for you. Additionally, your management company will expect you to maintain a regular practice schedule and always be working on new material.

It is also not your manager's job to manage your finances or the band's finances. Your manager is not your accountant or your tax advisor. Paying your bills and the band's bills is your responsibility. If the band is established enough, you can hire a business manager to be responsible for these functions. Of course, if your contract with your management company gives the manager the right to incur expenses that are to be paid by the band, the manager does have to provide you with an accounting and any other necessary documentation for those costs.

A frequent misconception about the role of managers involves the booking of shows and finding other musical employment opportunities. Many musicians new to the music business think their manager should be finding and booking shows for them to play. This is not the role of the manager—in fact, it is generally considered to be a legal conflict of interest for your manager to book shows. Finding employment and booking it is not a management function—it is the function of a talent or booking agent. Your manager's role is to help you decide what opportunities to seek and which offers to accept. This is part of the manager's role as your advisor. The actual booking of the show must be handled separately by the booking agent. (Booking shows and the role of the booking agent are discussed in Chapter 5.)

PAYING YOUR MANAGER

Most management companies work on a percentage basis. Generally, the management company will receive a percentage of everything you make from your music career. That means that they will be entitled to money from shows you play, as well as merchandise and CDs you sell. If you get a recording contract, your management company is entitled to a commission on those proceeds as well.

The amount of this percentage is negotiated in the contract. It will generally be somewhere between 15% and 25%, with 20% being average. Saying that the percentage is negotiable, while technically true, may not be the case as a practical matter for new bands. Most management companies have a standard percentage that they require and will not negotiate this percentage down unless you are a well-established band with a significant income stream in place.

This may seem like a hard-line approach to the musician, especially when you are not making much money from your music career as it is. But, from the company's side, the non-negotiable percentage is based on the economics of working with a less-established band on which the company makes very little money. The management company has to devote its time and resources to your band and still make enough money to pay the management company's bills and have some level of profitability. The music industry is highly competitive, and most bands never get beyond the local or regional scene. That means that the management company is taking a big chance when they sign on a band that is not established and does not have a record deal. Starting out, they will not come close to making back their expenses out of the twenty percent they make off your shows. It is only when your band makes it to the next level that the management company can recoup its investment in your band.

If your band is one of the fortunate ones and you find success in the music business, you may eventually reach a point where the amount of money your band is making gives you enough clout to negotiate a reduction with your management company. If you find yourself in this position, you can expect any reduction in the company's standard percentage to be based on income levels achieved by the band. For instance, you may be able to negotiate a provision that says that you will pay the management company 20% of everything you make up to some amount of money, at which point the percentage reduces to 15%. However, you will have to wait until either you have some reasonable expectation of reaching those levels in the very near future or have been a good client of the company to negotiate such a deal. If the company agrees to include a provision of this type in your contract before you have anything on the horizon, you can expect the point at which the percentage reduction is triggered to be fairly high.

Exclusion from Commissions

Generally, the manager's percentage will apply to all of the monies you make as a result of your music career—live performance fees, recording fees, profits from merchandise, and publishing monies received. However, you should be sure that any management agreement you sign also sets out some limitations on monies that you may receive that should not be subject to the management fee.

For example, say that you are headlining the show and are responsible for getting the opening and support bands for that bill. The venue is paying you a sum of money for that night's show and requires that you be responsible for paying the bands you have hired to play with you that night. The money you receive for the venue that is paid out to the other bands should not be subject to a management fee by your management company. Therefore, you will want to be sure that funds you receive that are to be paid out to third parties are specifically excluded from gross earnings in your management contract. The same is true for things like sound and light costs for live performances and *deficit tour support* (money you receive for tour funding that has to be paid back to your label if it is part of your record deal). Costs you pay for recording should also be excluded from the commissions received from those recordings.

Post-Term Commissions

You should expect to see a section on post-term commissions in the contract. Once your contract with the management company has ended (or, for some other reason, you and your management company have parted ways), there will be circumstances in which the management company will still be entitled to receive its management fee from you. For example, if you record masters during the term of your management contract, and those masters are later used (generally referred to in the industry as *exploiting the masters*), then your management company will get its full percentage from the exploitation of those masters—regardless of whether the contract is still in effect.

Be sure, however, that there is some time limitation on this clause in the contract. You should not be paying your manager commissions on everything for the rest of your career. Somewhere between six months and two years is reasonable, depending on the status of your career.

The management company will also want to be paid its percentage for opportunities that were arranged for you during the term of the agreement, even though the actual event occurred or monies were paid to you after the contract has ended. For this type of post-term commission, you want to have the management agreement set a time limit for how far into the future the full commissions are payable, and set out a sliding scale that reduces the percentage over time.

THE MANAGEMENT CONTRACT

Beyond the important provision of the amount of money you will have to pay the manager, a typical management agreement is several pages long and contains other equally important provisions.

Length of Contract

One of these provisions is the *term*, or length, of the contract. Any management agreement, or contract of any type for that matter, should contain a section that addresses how long the contract will be in effect.

Most management companies are going to want to sign you to an initial period of no less than one year, and very likely will ask for an even longer term. From the company's perspective, they do not want to invest a significant amount of time and money into your musical career only to have your contract expire and not be renewed. Of course, from the band's point of view, a shorter term may be preferable to a longer term, at least until you know how the manager-artist relationship is going to work out.

One way to negotiate this provision so that the needs of both parties are met is to set up a shorter initial period followed by a series of option years. The contract can be drafted so that the management company has an automatic option to renew if certain stated income goals are reached. Alternatively, the contract can contain a shorter initial period followed by an automatic renewal right, unless there are grounds to void this option right. Under no circumstances should you sign a contract for a period of longer than seven years. The laws in some states, such as California, say that a contract for a term longer than seven years is not enforceable; but even more importantly, a longer-term contract is too long a time period to be in the artist's best interest.

There have been management companies whose contracts were not drafted to run for a specific period of time, but rather for an album cycle. For example, such a contract might have stated that the management contract would last until seven albums had been released. The way the recording industry operates, that type of contract could potentially tie a band to a management company for an indefinite period of time. These types of contracts have now fallen out of favor and are even prohibited by law in some states. Therefore, if you are presented with a management agreement with this type of provision, you should either renegotiate to a specific amount of time for the term or consider finding a different management company. You may want to obtain the assistance of an attorney if you find yourself in this situation.

Duties of the Manager

Your management contract should also contain a section setting out the duties your manager is undertaking. The language in this section may state something to the effect of:

> (Your manager) *agrees to advise, counsel, and direct you in matters relating to your professional career, in areas such as the selection of material, publicity and marketing, compensation, and other general practices in the entertainment industry.*

Additionally, the manager's duties may include helping you pick the other people to be on your team, such as other musicians and your booking agent.

Authority of Manager

Management contracts often contain a section setting out what actions the manager is authorized to take on your behalf. Items that may appear in this section include the authorization to approve publicity and advertising, including the use of your name and photograph. There may also be a section authorizing the management company to sign contracts on your behalf. Generally, this section should be limited to signing basic contracts, such as performance agreements for short-term engagements (less than three days).

You and the management company can negotiate whether the things your manager is authorized to do may be done without consulting you. On the other end of this spectrum, your management contract may specify that your manager is authorized to do these things only after you have agreed to them in writing, although this is much less common and is not always a practical way of doing things.

Along those same lines, the contract should also contain provisions that set out the extent of the management company's authority to incur expenses that the artist must pay.

Generally, these expenses include things like travel expenses, advertising and publicity expenses, and phone and delivery tolls. Be warned—make sure the contract is clear that the band does not pay any of the manager's regular office overhead.

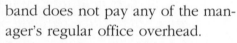

Musical Note

Most management companies will require the artist to pay the costs associated with the management of the band. This is in addition to the commissions the management company is paid.

As an artist, you will want to maintain some control over your expenses so that they do not get out of hand. It is always a wise move to have limits set in the contract as to how much of your money the management company can spend without consulting you in advance. You will probably want to authorize your manager to spend a pre-set amount each month without your prior authorization, just as a convenience to both of you. It can get tiresome if your manager has to get your approval on every single expense item, no matter how small it may be. However, you should be wary of giving your manager a blank check to spend your money, as this can cause you to lose control of your business funds completely.

As a new band, allowing the management company to spend $200-$500 per month without consulting you is probably acceptable. As your career becomes more established and your expenses go up, you may want to set this number at a higher level if your experiences with the management company in this area have been positive. Of course, your management company should provide you with an accounting of all of your funds that they have expended and should be able to provide you with documentation to verify any monies they expect you to pay.

Along those same lines, be careful about management contracts that give your manager complete *power of attorney authority*. This allows the manager to do everything as though he or she were you. You may want the manager to have some authority, but there should be some limitations on that authority.

Canceling the Contract

It is also important to have some sort of *out clause* in the contract. There should be some things that are considered significant breaches of the management agreement, which should allow the innocent party to cancel the contract. If you are signing a long-term contract, you may want to have provisions that allow you to get out of the contract if you do not reach certain income levels. You will want to include a clause in the contract stating that, if your manager has a pattern of failing to get your approval for things when the contract requires him or her to do so, you have the right to terminate the contract.

Understand What You are Signing

Before you sign a management contract presented to you by a management company, be sure you understand all of terms in the contract. Once you sign and become a member of the *management company family*, your manager should be looking out for your best interest. It is important for you to remember that, until you sign the agreement, you are not yet a member of the family. At this point in the relationship, the management company is looking out for its interest, and they expect you to be responsible for looking out for yourself.

The management company likely has a lawyer who has written its standard management agreement and who will be responsible for negotiating the management contract with you. That lawyer represents only the management company and cannot give you legal advice. It is a good idea to hire your own attorney to help you with the negotiation process, or at a minimum, to go over the contract with you. However, be sure that you consult with an attorney who has experience in entertainment law, particularly with the music industry.

There are certain ways that things in the music industry are done, and an entertainment lawyer with be familiar with those industry standards. A lawyer who practices in another area will not be familiar with the industry, and this lack of knowledge about the way the music business works and about what a management contract should and should not say can seriously affect your negotiations with the management company. Hiring the wrong lawyer can bog down the process to the point that the management company may lose interest in signing you at all. (Review Chapter 6 for tips on how to find and work with the right attorney.)

FIRING YOUR MANAGER

If you want to end the contract and do not really have grounds to do so, you can try to negotiate an agreed *release* from the contract with your manager or management company. If the company will release you from the contract, you should get some sort of written agreement from them that grants you the release and sets out the terms of your agreement related to the termination of the contract. If there is no breach of the contract and the company will not agree to the release, you will have to consult an attorney if you have any hope of ending the contract. Either way, you may be stuck until the end of the contract period.

Beyond the legalities of terminating your management contract, you should give some serious thought before firing your manager. The manager you choose can have a significant impact on the success you ultimately achieve. Having connections to the right people and putting you in the right place at the right time all are factors in helping you achieve success. However, there are limits to what your manager can do for you, and some things are beyond his or her control.

Also, be sure you are being realistic about whether your manager is working for you or not. Ultimately, it is the material that gets an artist noticed. If they are submitting your material and working to promote your band, but you are not achieving the success you think you should, remember that it may not be the manager's fault. You should consider whether your material is really as good as you think it is and listen carefully to what industry professionals tell you about it. A manager can submit your material, but cannot force a record label to sign you or a radio station to play your songs.

Failure to reach the top may not mean you just need to change managers, and it is important to be realistic about where you began, where you are now, and where you hope to go. Make the best choices you can for your career. If you have a bad experience with management, learn from the mistakes you both made and apply those lessons in your search for new management.

DO'S AND DON'TS

Finally, here are some do's and don'ts for doing business with a manager or management company. Be professional and business-like when you deal with them. If your manager calls you, be sure to return the call. Show up to meetings on time, and don't miss or be late to shows.

Keep your manager abreast of everything that could affect your career and your availability to perform. Family problems can easily translate into band problems, so let your manager know about issues like this before they get out of hand. Also, be realistic about the impact your family obligations have on your career. If you have small children at home, will you be able to perform in shows and go out of town, or will this curtail your career options? It is difficult to support family on the money you make touring with a band.

If you are presented with any opportunity, whether it is as significant as a record deal or as minor as an offer to play at a friend's birthday party, never accept the offer without discussing it with your manager.

chapter four:
Business Managers

The previous chapter focused on the personal manger—the one who gives you career advice. While some of the advice the personal manager gives you is related to finances, such as how much you can expect to be paid for particular activities in the music industry, a personal manager is not a financial manager or business manager. The business manager is the person responsible for the management of your money once it has been earned.

WHAT THE BUSINESS MANAGER DOES

Business managers provide basic accounting services, and should be able to let you know exactly how much money you have earned and from what sources. They should also keep track of your expenses. Depending on what contractual arrangements you have with your business manager, he or she may also be responsible for paying your monthly bills for you. If you have this arrangement, you will have to decide whether to authorize your business manager to sign your checks for you or not. It should go without saying that, before you permit a business manager or anyone else to write checks on your bank account, you have to be absolutely certain that person is trustworthy.

Everyone has seen media reports of celebrities who earn enough money to be very wealthy ending up in bankruptcy court because they did business with an unprofessional business manager and lost control of their finances. To avoid that problem, many artists set their business up so that they sign each and every check themselves. While this may seem like a great deal of trouble and may be inconvenient when you are on the road on tour, it is the best way to ensure that you know what is going on with your money. Oprah Winfrey has said on her show that she signs all of her checks herself. If she can find the time for this, so can you.

Stay in Control

If your business manager is paying all of your bills for you, it is still important for you to keep up with your finances. You should always know how your money is being spent. At the same time, you need to make sure you and your band are operating within your financial means. There is a temptation to live your life as though that money will come in at those levels forever, especially when you reach a level that brings in a substantial amount of money for you.

As you begin to make money, you will also find that so-called friends of yours will start appearing. The smart artists are the ones who are best able to distinguish between genuine friends and people who are interested only in either hanging out with a celebrity or in separating you from your money.

As you start making money, you will be offered all kinds of investment opportunities. Analyze each one carefully. It is at these times that a competent business manager can be a big help to you. These things are all part of managing your money well. Unless you are extremely fortunate, you will have a limited window of time during which you will earn most of your money from your musical career. Even though it seems like it is too far in the future to even consider, you should establish retirement accounts if you are fortunate enough to make a lot of money in the music business. If you act wisely now, you can secure your financial future. If you fail to do so, you run the risk of becoming one of the sad stories of musicians who were rich as young people but broke by the time they reached middle age.

SELECTING A BUSINESS MANAGER

Because the financial decisions you make now will, at least to some degree, impact you for the rest of your life, you must be sure the person or company you select as your business manager is professional and competent. There are not any legal requirements or licensing rules for business managers. It is critically important for you to check out the qualifications of a proposed business manager. Is the person you are considering hiring a *certified public accountant*? Many people think that all business managers are CPAs, but this is not the case. If he or she is not, find out what experience and qualifications he or she does have. Ask for references.

If the business manager is giving you investment advice, you need to know whether they are licensed or not. Federal law requires people who are giving investment advice (for example, which stocks and bonds to buy) to have a license. You should also find out whether the business manager is receiving referral fees or commissions for directing you to any investments.

You should also know for certain that basic things, like preparing and filing income tax returns, are done in a timely manner. Even if you have a professional business manager, the federal law still makes the final responsibility yours. If your tax returns are not properly and timely filed, you will be the one in trouble with the authorities.

PAYING YOUR BUSINESS MANAGER

You must decide how you will pay your business manager. Many managers will work on some sort of hourly fee or will charge for services as they are rendered. If you are hiring a manager to work on an hourly basis, be certain that you have a clear understanding of what services the manager is performing and what the hourly rate is. If you fail to do this, you may be in for a very large surprise when the bill arrives. Also, remember that if you are hiring a manager on a limited basis, the manager is not handling all of your business—only what you hired him or her to do. You are responsible for knowing what the manager is doing and what responsibilities you still have.

You may also be able to hire a manager on a flat monthly fee basis. Under this scenario, you will pay the manager a set amount each month. In return, the manager will perform a set list of functions for you. For example, the manager may do your basic accounting for you and keep track of the monies you are paid. The flat fee may include the manager paying a certain number of bills for you each month. You will be responsible for everything else.

The final method of paying a manager is the percentage method. Some managers will handle all of the business affairs for your band (or your musical career if you are a solo artist) for a fixed percentage of all the money you make. Five percent is the average charge.

THE RELATIONSHIP

In addition to coming to an agreement on how the business manager will be paid, you and the manager should have an agreement on the ground rules for your relationship. You must know what kind of communications to expect from the manager. You should receive regular financial reports from the manager, and you need to have established deadlines for the receipt of these reports. You also need to know what the manager's rules and policies are regarding providing documentation to you and allowing you to audit the books. If a manager will never allow you to audit the books or receive any back-up information, this may be a red flag about the quality of the manager you have chosen. This is your money—you need to know exactly where it is going. If there are things in the reports your business manager provides that you do not understand, ask for clarification. If your reports are never explained to your satisfaction, and you cannot account for your money and how it has been spent, it is probably time to find a new business manager.

chapter five:
Doing Business
with Booking Agents

Another important member of your team is the *booking agent*, also known as the *talent agent*. As previously discussed, the management team is responsible for advising the artist on his or her musical career, but not for actually securing employment for the artist. It is the booking agent who fills this role.

As a band just starting out, you have probably been doing all of your own booking, so you know what a time-consuming process it is to contact clubs and arrange for shows. The music business being what it is, you have undoubtedly experienced having shows canceled at the last minute, having the line-up changed at the last minute, and having other bands not show up. You may have worked hard to get booked into a club, only to end up playing with other bands whose musical style does not mesh with yours. This can be a problem if the styles are so far apart that each band's fans hate the other band's music.

Depending on your hometown and your genre of music, you may have had trouble even getting paid for the shows you play. Many clubs, especially in places with active local music scenes, are reluctant to pay new bands until the band has established a reputation for being able to bring out people to the club and hold on to the people already there.

WHAT A BOOKING AGENT DOES

Over time, a band can work hard and establish a good reputation in its hometown and overcome most or all of the normal problems on their own. However, it does take a long time and it requires a great deal of work on the band's part. Hiring a booking agent can be a definite help in this area. A good booking agent will be able to get you booked into the venues that are best suited to your music, help you break into the best local venues, and help you get paid for your shows. Your booking agent will know the going rate for venues in your area and for bands that play your type of music. The booking agent should also be able to help you get good bills, so that you are playing with bands that fit well with you and that already have an established fan base. This can help you broaden your own fan base and improve your draw at the local clubs.

For a local band in the early part of its musical career, it can also be difficult to get shows in cities beyond your local area. The venues in the other areas do not know you or your music, and are hesitant to book unknown acts. If you are working with a booking agent, he or she will be able to help you get these shows, because they will have already established good working relationships with the talent agents for the venues in many cities.

FINDING A BOOKING AGENT

As with managers, there are local booking agencies and large national agencies, and the same situation exists with the national booking agencies as with management firms. You will find it very hard to get a big, national agency to book you when you are a new band just starting out. They are looking for more established bands who have already reached a significant earnings level. That means that you will be working with a smaller agent, at least initially. You should apply the same criteria to hiring your booking agent that you did for hiring a manager—find someone with a good reputation who has the ability to get your band the shows it deserves.

You also need to know what qualifications your booking agent has. In some states, there are no licensing or education requirements for booking agents, so be sure you are working with a reputable agent. If you are hiring a booking agent whose office is in a state that does require licensing and registration, you can verify the status of an agent you are thinking of hiring with the regulatory authorities in that state.

REVIEW AND UNDERSTAND YOUR AGREEMENT

If the agent has you sign a contract making them the exclusive booking agent for your band, be sure you have an attorney review the contract for you. You should also keep the contract period relatively short so that you are not stuck with a bad booking agent for a long period of time. The same rules about firing your manager apply to firing your booking agent. If you have a contract, then the terms of that contract control. If the booking agent is not in breach of the agreement, the only way you can end the contract prior to its expiration is by getting the agent to agree to end the relationship. Get a written release from the agent if this happens.

Booking agents normally work on a percentage of the fee you earn for your performance. In reviewing your contract, make sure it is clear that the agent is only receiving a percentage of the income you make from performing. Your booking agent is not part of the recording or publishing process, and therefore, should not be entitled to any money from these income sources. The fees vary and can range anywhere from 10% to 25% for nonunion musicians in unregulated states.

Of course, this situation is completely different if you are a member of one of the unions. There are several unions that can come into play for musicians—the *American Federation of Musicians* (AFM), *American Federation of Television and Radio Artists* (AFTRA), *the Screen Actor's Guild* (SAG), and *Equity*. If you are a union member, the rules require you to work only with an authorized talent agent who has agreed to abide by the union's restrictions. The union will set an upper limit of 10% on the amount charged by the booking agent.

In some states, such as Texas, very few local musicians are union members. In other states, the unions have a very strong presence. Most musicians who work in these states will end up being members. There may be no need to join a union right away; however, as your career grows and expands, that need may change. The savvy musician knows the rules in his or her own geographic location, and makes decisions and changes based on the track of his or her career. (A sample of a contract with a booking agency is included in the Appendix, p.203.)

TIPS FOR WORKING WITH YOUR BOOKING AGENT

To make the most out of your relationship with your booking agent, follow some of these tips. Be professional when it comes to showing up for your gigs. Don't cancel, especially at the last minute, unless you have a very good reason for doing so. This makes your band, your manager, and booking agent look bad. Be on time, including being on time for the load-in. As with your manager, keep your booking agent advised of any issues that could affect your availability for shows. When you have times that your band is not available for shows, tell your agent as soon as you know so that he or she won't waste time trying to book you during that period.

Pay your bill. Not paying your agent can get you a bad reputation, especially on the local scene when you are trying to get your career started. Don't agree to shows on your own, either. Always go through the agent. If you don't, you may end up ruining a good opportunity somewhere else that the agent has lined up for you or end up double booked on a date. And remember, the booking agent is just that—he or she books shows for you. They are not your management company, and you cannot expect them to give you the same career and business advice as a manager will.

chapter six:
Doing Business with Attorneys

Another critical member of your band's team is the lawyer. You may believe that you do not need to deal with an attorney, especially as a young band just starting out. In fact, you may be able to manage on your own without one. However, this presumes that you are fortunate enough to always be dealing with reputable management companies, booking agents, and venues. You will also have to do a competent job managing the business aspects of your band, and have the ability to understand what a contract says and where the pitfalls are. If you are unsuccessful in any of these areas, and your band achieves any degree of success, you will very likely reach the point at which you regret not hiring an attorney at the beginning to help you with the legal issues surrounding your career.

THE ROLE OF THE ATTORNEY

An attorney representing a band will likely be involved in many areas of the band's career as it develops. As your band gets started, you will need an organizational structure. A smart band that plans on making music a career will take care of this issue early in the life of the band.

The different organizational structures your band can take are discussed in Chapter 1. In addition to giving you advice as to which structure best meets the band's needs, it is the attorney who will help you execute the plans you make. Attorneys can draft partnership agreements for the band or do the paperwork necessary to incorporate the band. Your lawyer can also help devise the contracts that govern the terms of each band member's employment with the band. Issues relating to the ownership of the band's name and the material written by various members can also be put into written form by the lawyer. Taking care of these issues at the beginning solves many problems later.

While you can do these things yourselves, it requires an investment of time and research to learn what you need to do and how to do it. If you are like most musicians who are starting out, you will find it difficult to devote the necessary time to these activities. They will end up way down on your priorities list—somewhere after maintaining your day job, practicing with the band, writing new material, and booking your own shows.

An entertainment lawyer will also be able to help you trademark the band's name so that you own the rights to the name. The importance of taking this step cannot be overstated, as many bands on the verge of some broader popularity have been forced to change their name because someone else already owned the name they were using. This can stop a band in its tracks. Using an attorney will make this process easier.

 Musical Note

Many musicians have been trapped in bad contracts because they were mistaken about what they thought they were agreeing to in the contract.

Should your band be fortunate enough to be offered a record contract, you will definitely want to hire a lawyer. There are many complex issues that go into such deals. Record company contracts can be long, difficult documents, especially when you are dealing with the major and mini-major labels. Do not try to negotiate one of these deals on your own. (More on record deals is discussed in Chapter 12.)

However, you may want to hire a lawyer not just to help you with the contract once you have received an offer from a label, but to help you get the offer in the first place. There are entertainment attorneys who will shop your material for you, and many of them have good connections and can help you get signed. If you are thinking about this kind of deal with your lawyer, be sure you have a clear understanding of what the attorney is and is not agreeing to do for you. Also, be sure you understand the fee structure to which you are agreeing.

FINDING AN ATTORNEY

Finding the right attorney for your needs can be an intimidating task. There are pages and pages of listings for lawyers in the phone book, and it can be hard to know where to start. The most important thing to keep in mind as you begin your search is that you are looking for an *entertainment attorney*. While any licensed attorney can review a contract for you and help you negotiate terms to put in it, a lawyer who is not familiar with the music industry may not know what belongs in each kind of contract and what does not. A specialist will also know where the traps are in a contract. This is particularly important as your career advances and you begin dealing with the big players in the music business.

Before you discuss any of your situation in detail, ask the lawyer if he or she will have any conflicts of interest in representing you. Attorneys ethically cannot represent both sides to a transaction (like a contract negotiation). Before you discuss the specifics, you need to know that the attorney you are thinking of hiring to represent you in the review of a management contract does not already represent the management company.

Musical Note

Be sure that your entertainment lawyer has experience in the music business. He or she may be a great lawyer for actors or athletes, but that does not mean he or she knows anything about the music world.

One way to find an entertainment attorney is to get to know other local musicians and get a referral from them. If you live in a large city, there may be a local bar association that maintains a referral list. Check to see if your state has a music office or music directory—if it does, it may have a listing of entertainment lawyers. Of course, there is always the Internet. A search for "entertainment attorneys" will get you a listing of attorneys, or you can use one of the commercial referral sites such as **www.legalmatch.com**.

Once you have found some prospective attorney, you should interview and screen them. Ask about their experience in the music business. A competent attorney should willingly answer these questions. If your attorney is going to be shopping your record, be sure to ask for references. You want to know what success that person has in getting deals for clients. When you get the references, check them out. Call the other musicians and see how happy they are with the work done by the attorney, and whether or not the lawyer actually did secure a record deal for them.

You can also check with the bar association in the state where the attorney practices to see if he or she has ever been disciplined. Attorneys are subject to rules and regulations that govern their conduct, and a lawyer is disciplined when the state bar association finds that he or she has violated these rules. If the attorney you are thinking of hiring has been in a lot of trouble with the bar association, you might want to keep looking for another lawyer.

PAYING YOUR LAWYER

There are two main ways attorneys get paid for their work. One is the hourly fee and the other is the percentage. Each of these works generally as you would expect. In an hourly arrangement, you pay the lawyer a set amount per hour and are billed for everything the attorney does for you. Hourly rates vary widely, depending on your geographic location and the experience level of the attorney. The best known music lawyers can go for more than $500 per hour. Lawyers who work on a percentage get their percentage of everything you make, which is generally 5%.

There is a third method of billing called *value billing*. In this method, the attorney sets the amount of the fee based on the attorney's contribution to the project for which he or she was hired. The problem with this method is that there is no magic formula to determine what the fee amount totals at the end. If you are entering into a value billing deal, learn as much as you can about what factors determine the fee and try to get a written commitment of an estimated range for the fee.

Regardless of which method your lawyer uses, you will have to pay any *costs*. For instance, if your band incorporates, the state will charge a fee to issue your corporate charter, and you will have to pay this cost. This is an addition to the fees paid to the attorney for the work done.

THE WORKING RELATIONSHIP

Once you have hired an attorney, you have to maintain a good working relationship with the person you hired. Your attorney should generally keep you informed about what he or she is doing for you. For example, if you have received an offer from a record label, the attorney should keep you in the loop during the negotiation process. It is important for you to respond quickly and professionally to your attorney when he or she asks you for information or for a decision. If your lawyer's office has to keep calling you and trying to track you down, you are wasting everyone's time. If you do not return phone calls or are too hard to work with, the attorney may decide he or she no longer wants you as a client.

If you become dissatisfied with your lawyer, you can terminate the attorney/client relationship. If you have a written contract with your lawyer, be sure you understand what the termination requirements are, and in the case of a percentage arrangement, what the terms are in regard to that percentage after the contract ends. When you fire your lawyer, be sure you do so in writing. Send the attorney a letter by certified mail, return receipt requested, telling him or her you are ending the attorney/client relationship. You should keep a copy of this letter for your own records.

chapter seven:
Equipment Issues

As a musician, you undoubtedly own equipment that you use when you perform. These include the obvious things, like musical instruments and amplification tools, and less obvious things, like the vehicle you use to get to the performance itself. There are a few issues in this area—generally related to liability—that merit discussion.

PAYING FOR EQUIPMENT

If you are a solo artist, the issue is clear—you already know that you are responsible for paying for whatever you buy, and once it is paid for, you own it. If you are in a group, there are additional factors at play.

A band operating without a formal written agreement is considered a partnership. The band members need to be aware of this fact when equipment is purchased. If general band funds are used (money made by the band before distribution to the individual members), then the equipment belongs to the partnership. This is true even if the equipment is an instrument used by only one member of the group. If that member leaves the group, the equipment stays with the group unless the band agrees otherwise. The same is true if the band is incorporated. Equipment bought with corporate funds belongs to the corporation and not the individual band members.

If the equipment is going to be bought on credit, there are liability issues you must consider before borrowing any money. If the money is borrowed in the name of the partnership, then each of the individual members can be held responsible for paying off the loan. Even if only one of the band members signs for the loan, the other members may still be responsible for the debt. That is how partnership laws generally work.

Musical Note

If you have a formal partnership agreement, you should address how equipment will be paid for and who owns it.

If the band is incorporated and the loan is strictly in the corporate name, then the individual band members are not liable for the debt. This is another benefit of incorporating. However, many companies will not extend credit to new corporations with no corporate credit history. In those situations, they may ask for a *personal guarantee*. If that happens, the person who signs the guarantee is then personally responsible for paying the debt if the corporation defaults and does not pay. The members of the band who did not sign the guarantee are not responsible.

If the debt is not paid by either the partnership or corporation, and the individual members are liable, your personal assets can be taken to pay off this debt. In some states, your paycheck from any job you hold can be *garnished* (some amount of money will be withheld every pay period and paid to the creditor) and your house, if you own one, can be taken. Therefore, before the band borrows money to purchase something, each member should be aware of what obligations he or she is personally taking on.

LIABILITY CONCERNS

Liability may also be incurred as a result of the use of equipment. If you have an equipment stack onstage, and you or the band's set up crew stack it incorrectly and it falls, the band and the individual members could be sued by anyone who was hurt when the stack fell. Many new bands who are not yet established will not have insurance to cover this problem, and the individual members' personal assets could be taken to pay for the damages.

Items you use in your stage show that cause damage to either the venue or to fans can also cost you money. If some of your electrical equipment shorts out and causes a fire, the band could be held responsible for the damages. Most venues will have insurance to cover events like this, but some smaller events may not. Further, the venue's insurance may not protect you—even if it pays for the damage, the venue's insurer can go after you to recover what it paid on your behalf.

VEHICLES

The use of vehicles can also result in liability for the band or its individual members. Depending on how the laws in the state where an incident occurs are drafted, a band member could end up being financially responsible if another member of the band or a band crew member has a wreck and hurts someone on the way to or from a show. If you are hauling band equipment in your vehicle or in a trailer attached to your vehicle, you should be sure that you have adequate insurance coverage in case you are involved in an accident. Even if you are not the owner of the vehicle in the wreck and were not even present when the wreck occurred, you could still end up being personally liable.

WHAT YOU NEED

What kind of equipment you need for your shows depends on what type of music you play. If you are a solo pianist or acoustic guitar player playing in a restaurant, you will not need the same set of equipment as a rock band playing in a club.

Bands playing stage shows may want to purchase their own sound equipment. This equipment includes the microphones and stands as well as the sound board. If you have a sound board, you may also want to hire a sound engineer once you can afford it. Especially in smaller clubs, the venue may not provide an engineer and you will have to adjust the levels yourselves before you begin to play and they will stay the same throughout your set when done this way.

 Musical Note

If you own your own sound equipment, always bring all of it to every show—no matter what the venue tells you it has available. You never know when a part may break or be missing. If the sound equipment doesn't work, your show won't go on.

You can also consider buying your own lights and light controls. You can hire someone to work your lights or you can buy equipment that has auto switching features. Some of these work on a regular rotation schedule while others work off of the sound levels.

Fog machines and other special effects items may also be part of your equipment list. If there is any question about what special effects you plan on using, be sure to check with the venue first to be sure you can use them.

Also, when you come to play a show, be sure to bring things like duct tape to tape down all the electrical cords. You will also want plastic ties to hold your banners and mic cords.

As you become able to afford more and better equipment, you can consider purchasing insurance in case the equipment is damaged. You will need to evaluate how much the insurance costs and what things it will actually pay for and compare that to the amount of money it would cost to replace everything without the insurance.

chapter eight:
The Business of Performing

One of the primary activities in which you will be engaged as a professional musician is performing in public. Whether you are playing your own music or songs written by someone else, there are numerous issues involved—both in setting up the performance and in the performance itself.

SETTING UP A SHOW

As a musician just starting out, the hardest part of setting up a show may be getting a venue to allow you to play. You will start this process by determining which venues in your local area have live music that is of the same general type, or *genre*, as yours. The next step is to contact the venue and find out who handles the talent booking for them. You can do this by calling the venue directly, but you may also want to go online. If the venue has a website, it may give you information about how and where to submit your material.

If you have recorded a CD, the talent agent will want you to send them the CD and a press pack. A press pack is used to send to clubs and radio stations to introduce your band to talent buyers for venues and program directions for radio play.

The press pack should contain a photo of the band, a short bio about the band members, and a description of the type of music you play. If you have received any sort of reviews in any publications, you should include those quotes. You should also include a list of your basic equipment and requirements for stage set-up. While you do not have to spend a fortune creating this press kit, the more professional it is in appearance, the better the impression you will make with the talent agent. Be sure both the press kit and the CD have the name of your band, as well as the names and phone numbers to contact for booking.

You can also use an electronic press kit, which allows people to view your press kit online. A press kit like this should contain everything previously mentioned for a regular press kit, but also have audio and video clips of the band and your set list (which has the songs you play with the lengths of each song listed also). You can set up an electronic press kit with Sonicbids at **www.sonicbids.com**.

If you have not recorded any of your songs, you can look around for venues that host *new band nights* or try to be included in a *battle of the bands*. However, you should also work on getting some type of recording. At this point, it does not have to be an expensive recording done in a studio with a producer. There are software programs available that will allow you to do to your own recording. It is not necessary to create a full length CD at this point—all you are trying to do is give the talent agents a good idea of how your band sounds. You really only need about four songs to accomplish this. Pick what you think are your strongest, most representative songs for this CD. If you are planning on performing original music, you should record songs your band has written and not any *cover songs* (songs written by others).

You will also need to have enough material ready. How much you will need depends on where you will be playing. If you are a cover musician and will be playing in a restaurant or bar, you may need to be able to play several *sets* over a two- to three-hour period. If you are a rock band playing on a bill with several other bands, you will need to have enough music to do a *set*. This set will be somewhere between thirty minutes and one hour.

Just remember as you try to find venues for shows, that it is very difficult to get slots in the best clubs in any city right away. It is also always difficult to break into the markets in the hot areas like Los Angeles, New York, Nashville, and Austin. There is a great deal of competition for the available slots, and the talent buyers in those markets do not often take chances on new, untested bands.

Negotiating the Gig

Once you have gotten a venue to give you a slot, the next step is to negotiate the terms of your performance. The word *negotiate* is used loosely here, because as a new band, you will not have any real negotiating power. In fact, you will be lucky to get paid any money for your performance. If you do get paid, it will be a very small amount—maybe $50 or $100.

To some extent, how you get paid will depend on where you are playing. The industry standards are different in different cities. In Los Angeles, not only should you expect not to be paid, but you should expect to be required to pay to play in most clubs. In Denver, many of the clubs do not charge covers to enter the club, and they will give you tickets to your show for you to sell. You will get paid based on the number of tickets you sell. In other places, you may be asked to play for free at first, then begin getting paid your second or third time to play that club.

In addition, you will want to nail down the other specifics of your performance—what time you will be going on, when the *load-in* is, and who will be responsible for the sound and lights. This last issue can be important, because you do not want to get to the club for your show only to find out that the club expects you to pay for the sound engineer or to have provided your own. If this happens to you, you will end up paying the club to play there or not being able to play at all. Many venues that regularly host live music will provide these items for you.

If possible, you should confirm the terms of your show in writing. This is generally done through a performance agreement, which is basically just a contract about your performance. Some local clubs may balk at signing a contract, but you may be able to at least get an email with the pertinent terms included. The contract should contain the basics—date and time of performance, amount of pay, when you will be paid, load-in time, set length, and the names of the venue and your band. Ideally, it will be signed by both the band and the booking agent for the club. If you are playing in a state where most musicians are unionized, the club may use the basic union contract form.

Another important item to include in a performance agreement—at least as your career advances—is the right to sell your merchandise at the concert. If you are playing in a club, the venue will probably allow you to keep all of the proceeds of the merchandise sales. However, you need to confirm this in the contract. For larger events (for example, shows in larger arenas set up by concert promoters), the venue may require you to pay them a percentage of the merchandise sales. When you reach this level, your booking agent, manager, and attorney will handle the negotiations on these contract provisions and will help you get the best deal possible. (A sample performance agreement is included in the Appendix, page 210.)

You may have heard people talk about *riders*. Riders are additions to the performance agreement that set out the extras for the band. These include things like food and drinks to be provided for the band, dressing room accommodations, local transportation needs, and other similar items. When you are starting out, your contracts will not have riders because you will not be getting any extras from the venues. As your band becomes more successful, you will be able to demand such things. When you get to that point, you will want to have your manager and attorney take care of creating the rider for your events. However, do not get too carried away with what you want in the rider. Until you get to be a major star with a strong demand for your services, if your rider is too extensive, you can lose shows because promoters will not want to deal with you and your demands.

GETTING PAID

There are several ways musicians traditionally get paid for their performances. One way is for the band to receive a *guaranteed fee*. This method works just how it sounds—the band and the venue agree in advance on a set fee that the band will receive. Sometimes, venues will pay a guarantee plus a possible bonus if you *draw well* that night. *Drawing well* means that your band brings out a good number of paying fans to the club.

Some clubs operate on a *scale*, which means they pay the band a set amount (for example, $3) per fan. Once your band reaches the level where you have a fairly predictable draw at shows at a particular venue, you may be able to receive a *percentage of the door*, or a percentage of the door with a guaranteed minimum payment. The *door* is the amount of money paid by patrons to come into the club.

If you are being paid based on your draw, the club is supposed to ask people as they come through the door which band they are there to see (assuming there is more than one band playing that night) and pay you based on the number of people who say they came to see your band. You will generally have to take the club's word for the count. The only way to challenge it is for you to have someone stationed at the door all night to keep your own count. Some clubs have better reputations in this area than others. You will just have to learn by trial and error (and by talking to other bands) how each club operates.

If you are being paid a percentage of the door, you receive a percentage of the total amount taken in by the club for concert admission, regardless of which band the patrons came to see. You are still in the same situation in regard to calculating the door—you are generally at the mercy of the venue to be honest with you about this number. You will only be able to successfully challenge extremely large discrepancies—for instance, if the club pays you based on thirty people, and you and your representatives counted two hundred people in the club at one time.

Musical Note

If you play in a restaurant or bar doing cover songs, some places will not pay you to play the show, but will let you have a tip jar and keep whatever people pay you in tips.

As your band achieves a national reputation, you may reach the point of being able to negotiate an advance payment from the venue or promoter for your appearance. It is common for bands to ask for half of the money to be paid up front. Your performance agreement should specify the due date if you are receiving the up-front guarantee. Your contract should also specify that you will receive the balance of all monies due to you at the close of the night. This is generally how clubs and small venues handle the payout. They will settle with all the bands when the final band has finished performing.

HOW MUCH WILL YOU MAKE?

Of course, how much you will make depends on the success of your band and what other obligations must be paid. It also depends on the type of music you play.

A young rock band just starting out will be fortunate to get a $100-$300 guarantee from a club, but may (over time) be able to make $2000 to $3000 for a headlining show with a good draw. A country act or cover band may be paid considerably more for the same length of performance. This is because country bands have a greater cross-over appeal than bands in other genres, and can draw bigger crowds. Cover bands are paid well because they generally play in restaurants and clubs in more affluent areas, draw an older crowd that spends more, and play longer performances of multiple sets over the evening.

As you get booked into larger arenas, the money you make goes up. The upper limits on your pay for a live performance depend on the drawing ability of your band (which, in turn, generally depends on the success of your CDs in the marketplace and the amount of radio play and promotion you are receiving). Of course, this likely means that you have a record deal of some sort and your label is expending money on your behalf for tour support and promotions. This money will be recouped by the label out of your earnings. *Recoup* is the industry term for the repayment to the record label of money they have advanced to create or promote your music.

Suffice it to say that just playing in big arenas and having a large *gross income* (the money you make before expenses are taken out) is not the same thing as having a lot of money left over to put into your own pocket at the end of the day.

Whether you are on your own or with a management company, you still need to promote your shows. This is another cost you will have to bear, but some venues may help with this expense. At least two weeks before the show, have posters up in the venue and flyers available. You also need to pass out as many flyers as you can in the area where the show will take place—do this yourself or through a *street team*. (see p.154.) You may also want to buy advertising in any local music publications to promote your appearance.

PERFORMING MUSIC YOU DID NOT WRITE

Many bands play during the set, or even record, music that was written by someone not in the band. Often, this is a song made famous by another group. Performing these covers requires the musician to consider the issues of copyright, performing rights societies, and licenses.

The general rule is that a person who writes a song (this includes the music and the lyrics) owns the copyright to that song and is entitled to be paid anytime someone plays that song. There are three performing rights societies in the United States and one group that is responsible for paying royalties on digital downloads. It is their job to collect the royalties (the money due as payment for the use of the song) for their members.

The two biggest performance rights societies are the *American Society of Composers, Authors, and Publishers* (commonly referred to as ASCAP) and *BMI*. These two

groups have open membership rules, which means that anyone who meets the membership requirements may apply and
will be accepted for membership. The third performance
rights society is SESAC, which is smaller because you must be
recommended for membership by a SESAC member to be
able to join.

Generally, to be eligible, you must have written a song that
has either been recorded for commercial release or performed in public. The recording requirement does not mean
that you must have a deal with a major label to join. You can
record a CD in your garage—as long as it is publicly distributed by being sold or given away at your shows, you will
meet the requirement. Once you are accepted for membership, you then register the individual songs you have written
for inclusion in the database.

BMI has offices that serve various regions. The offices are
located in Los Angeles, New York, Nashville, and in Europe.
They may be reached by phone at 212-586-2000 or online at
www.bmi.com. ASCAP also has various offices. You can
join by calling 800-95-ASCAP or by applying online at
www.ascap.com. (Remember, to join SESAC, you have to be
recommended by a current member.)

Which organization you join is up to you. Over the life of the
commercial exploitation of your
song, the financial aspects are just
about the same. BMI is a privately
owned company, while ASCAP is
member-owned and operated. You
have to pick one or the other, however. You cannot belong to more
than one at the same time.

 Musical Note

ASCAP, BMI, and SESAC handle performance royalties for
U.S. performances. Foreign
royalties are handled by each
individual country.

Once you become a member, the organization assumes responsibility for collecting money each and every time someone performs one of your registered songs. This is obviously a significant source of revenue. If you are a band performing a song written by someone else, the writer gets paid for the use of the song by your band just like he or she does if it is on the radio. The writer earns money every time you play the song. Does that mean when you play in a club, you have to send part of your fee off to the performing rights society?

Generally, the answer to that question is *no*. Most clubs and places that host live music have licenses from the performing rights societies, which allow the music to be played in the facility. The performing rights society collects the money due to the writer from the club.

Digital Performances

The performance rights societies do not collect royalties from digital transmissions of music. Music that is transmitted digitally, either on cable, satellite, or webcast, creates a royalty interest that is monitored and collected by *Sound Exchange*. You must register for membership with them separately from the other performing rights groups. You can join online at **www.soundexchange.com**. They pay their royalties in cycles, with registration deadlines that apply to each cycle. For example, the first deadline was scheduled to be July, 2005 for the first royalty cycle, covering 1996-2000. If you fail to register by the deadline, you will forfeit your accumulated royalties.

The Use of Written Music During a Performance

Some musicians, for example, pianists playing in a restaurant, may prefer to use sheet music when they perform. If you are in this category, you must remember that the person who wrote the sheet music has a copyright in that arrangement. If you display the sheet music when you perform, you violate the copyright in the arrangement if you do not have a license from the person who wrote that arrangement. Therefore, you should create your own arrangement. This is done by transcribing yourself the notes you will play in each song. Legally, this creates a new arrangement of the song in which you are the copyright holder. You may openly use your own arrangement without creating any copyright problems.

GOING ON TOUR

At some point in your musical career, you will face the issue of whether or not to go on tour. If you have signed a recording deal with a label (other than a small indie label), you will not have much of a decision to make. Your label will send you out on tour to support the album you are releasing. Prior to that point, however, the decision will be yours—as will the responsibility of setting up the tour.

Setting up a tour is a big job. You need promotional materials to use to get booked into the venues along the way. You have to know where those venues are and how to get a date there. You will either have to find gigs in several locations along the way or play close to your hometown so that you can get to the venue and back easily. You have to promote for the shows in those other cities, so you may need to hire a *street team* (an individual or group of people you hire to pass out flyers in advance of your show date). And you have to do all of this on a budget, because you will be making little or nothing for playing the shows on your tour as you are starting out.

You should have a goal in mind before you set up your tour. This process must start with knowing why you are going to play shows out of town. Are you trying to sell a CD you have recorded to fans in other cities? Are you trying to expand your fan base? If so, you have to prepare a plan for returning to play in those same cities. A one-time shot through a club will not help you to build much of a fan base in that city. It will take several trips.

You also have to consider the time you have available to do these multiple dates in out-of-town locations. At the start of your career, you will likely have a regular job that you will need to keep in order to support yourself. If your job schedule is such that you cannot get time off, your ability to go on a tour will be limited. Obviously, the distance you can travel from your home base for shows is also limited by your work schedule and your budget. In that instance, you will have to start slowly. For you, a tour may mean a weeklong set of dates every six to twelve months, or maybe just a series of long weekends. This type of touring will involve just stringing together dates at places you have already played and will be returning to in a few weeks to play again.

As your career advances, the length of your tours and the size of the venues into which you are booked will increase. This can happen slowly, as the result of careful planning and steady expansion of your fan base, or it can happen quickly, as the result of getting a record deal. While the fees you are able to command will increase, so will the potential problems and liabilities.

DEALING WITH LARGER VENUES

When you begin dealing with larger venues, you will need to have help from your team—especially your manager and attorney. The larger arenas will expect you to sign a written contract, and you must be absolutely certain that you understand the terms of this agreement. As you move into the larger venues, you will be able to negotiate advance payments for your shows. The general rule is for the advance to be about 50% of your total fee for each show.

At this career level, you should not negotiate the venue contract yourselves. If you do not have full-time team members in place, such as an attorney, a manager, and an agent, then you should consider at least hiring an attorney to help you negotiate this contract. This will help you get a better deal and protect you from any contract provisions that could result in an unpleasant surprise for the band at showtime.

Selling Your Merchandise

Playing a live show is an excellent opportunity to sell any merchandise you have available, such as CDs, T-shirts, hats, and other similar items. At the smaller venues, the clubs will generally let you sell your merchandise without charging you anything. As you move into the bigger venues, this will no longer be the case. The venues will charge you a fee for selling your merchandise. Generally, this will be a percentage of each item sold. The percentage is based on the sales price of the item, and will generally fall in the 30%–45% range.

Another issue that you need to address is who will be responsible for actually selling your merchandise. If you are dealing with a *merchandising company*, it will take care of resolving this issue for you. (see p. 156.) If you are still handling your own merchandise, then you need to know whether the venue is hiring the personnel to do the actual selling of your items or if you are responsible. The larger the venue, the more likely that it will provide the sales staff. At the club level, the venue usually does not provide any personnel for this purpose. If they do not provide the staff, then you will need to secure people to sell for you. This is a task you will need to handle in advance, especially when you are playing on the road and cannot just call your friends at the last minute or find some fans you know and trust at the show to handle the merchandise booth for you.

You will also need to create some sort of inventory control method. When you are still dealing with small amounts of merchandise early in your career, you do not need to have an incredibly complex system in place for this purpose. However, you do have to have a way to track how much merchandise (of each type) you brought to the show, what was sold, and how much money was made. You should create some sort of written system for this, because you will need this information when it is time to prepare the income tax return for the band. You are taxed on all money you made, including the money from the sale of merchandise. The costs you have incurred to create the things you have sold can be deducted from the total amount of money taken in from the sales (called the *gross receipts*) to get the taxable amount of income. If you do not have records about what was sold, how much you paid for it, and how much you got from the sale, you will not have the information you need to properly and accurately prepare your tax returns.

While you are handling your own merchandise, you are also responsible for getting it to and from the show. If there is a lot of merchandise and you are on an extended tour, you will have to arrange for shipping of your material to the various venues. This cost must be factored in when you set the sales prices for your various merchandise items.

When you are just starting out, you will most likely be securing your merchandise by paying for it up front and then selling it at some price set by the band so that a small profit is made. Of course, the fact that you are paying up front will limit the amount of merchandise you have available at any one time and the number of different items you can offer for sale. You will also be designing your own merchandise when your career is at this level, so you will have total control over the process.

Merchandising Companies

As you advance, this situation begins to change. For example, you may begin dealing with a *professional merchandising company*. This company will contract with you to create various items of merchandise to promote your band. From a legal perspective, this is accomplished by a contract that licenses the use of your band name and likeness (your pictures) to the merchandise company. The company designs the merchandise, makes sure it gets shipped to the various venues, and manages the financial aspects of the sales for you. You get paid by the merchandise company by receiving a royalty based on a percentage of the gross sales. The percentage you receive will be less than 50% and may be as low as 15% or 20%.

As with most other aspects of the music industry, the bigger your band is, the better the deal you get from the merchandise company will be. You will start out, more than likely, on the low end of the scale. Should you be fortunate enough to make it to the really big leagues, you may have enough power to negotiate a deal for royalty plus a percentage of the profits made by the merchandise company.

As a practical matter, you must have achieved some fairly decent level of success before a merchandise company will even be willing to do business with you. It costs the company money to produce the various items of merchandise, and they have to believe that they will be able to recoup their investment in your band and make a profit of some sort. They will want you to be selling out decent sized venues and may try to impose contractual requirements on you about the size of your shows.

Once again, this is the type of situation that is best handled by having an attorney to review and negotiate the merchandising contract. A merchandising contract may contain provisions for an advance against your future royalties and provisions for the repayment of the advance. These contract terms can become complex, and some of them have the potential to conflict with the terms and provisions of other contracts you may already have in place.

For example, you may have a contract with a merchandise company to place your material in retail outlets, with a provision making that merchandise company the exclusive sales outlet for your products in a particular city or country. If you then sign a contract with a different merchandiser to provide services for a specific tour, and that tour goes through the city or country covered by your exclusive retail merchandise contract, then your new contract for tour-related merchandise has a conflict with your existing contract.

If your new contract also has an exclusivity provision, then you have violated the terms of both contracts. You also need to consider any terms related to merchandise that may exist in your contracts with record companies to be sure the contract with the merchandise company does not conflict with the record contract. These are problems that an attorney who is familiar with all of your legal affairs and contracts should be able to spot and help you prevent.

PAYING FOR YOUR TOUR

Even if you have a record deal and are receiving tour support from your label, the band ultimately pays the costs associated with the tour. Some of the costs associated with the tour are obvious. For example, the band has to transport itself and its equipment to and from the performance. The members of the band and crew will have to eat while they are on the road. If the trip is of any distance, those people will need a place to sleep. How much you spend for each of these items is up to you, but you need to keep in mind that the more you spend on these things, the less money there will be for you at the end of the tour. You also have to determine, based on the venues in which you will be playing, whether you have to provide your own sound and lights. If you do, you will have increased personnel and travel costs.

Before you make decisions on these types of things, you need to discuss the overall economics of your tour with your team—particularly your manager and business manager. Your business manager can help you project how much money the band is likely to gross from the various tour dates, and can help calculate your expenses based on the different possibilities for accommodations, transportation, and other expenses. You also need to keep in mind as you are making these decisions that 100% of the money you make from your tour does not go into your pocket.

Once you have paid the basic costs of the tour, you still have to pay your manager, your attorney, your booking agent, and your business manager. It is easy for a band to get carried away on expenses and end up spending more than they make for the tour. Spending three or six months on tour and not having any money to put into your personal bank accounts when the tour is over can cause severe financial difficulties for each of the band members and their families.

Projecting Revenue

The primary factor in determining how your tour works out for you financially is how much money you are able to gross for the band from the tour. As a small band touring by playing dates in small venues and clubs, it is fairly easy to determine in advance what this amount will be. You are more likely to be getting paid a guaranteed amount or maybe a guarantee against a percentage of the door. This will give you some idea of what the final numbers will be. As your career progresses, these projections require more sophistication.

If you are renting venues to play your shows, you have to factor in the cost of the venue and calculate what the revenues from the door will be. You have to know how to deal with the variables of ticket pricing, which will now be determined by the band—in consultation with its team of advisors—and attendance levels. Unless you have specialized accounting training, you will have a difficult time being accurate enough in your projections. Failing to accurately project your numbers can result in an ugly bottom line.

You will also have to make projections on how much merchandise you will sell along the way, how much you will actually net from your projected sales, and how the tour will affect sales of your CDs. If you are on a tour in support of a new album, you have to keep in mind that you may not see any of the money from the CD sales, because your record contract may require you to repay recording and tour support and other costs before you see any actual cash. If you are in a venue that merits formally selling advance tickets, you will have to factor in the costs associated with printing and selling those tickets. You will have to go through a ticket service, and that will require you to pay some portion of the ticket price to the ticketing service.

Insurance

There are other costs associated with touring, and the bigger an act you are, the more of these costs you will incur. For instance, at some point before you do a significant amount of extended touring, you will need to obtain insurance. You will be traveling in vehicles that you own either as a band or individually, especially at the beginning of your careers, and these vehicles all have to have insurance. You may also need to have the individual band members covered by liability insurance and key man insurance, in case the band members either get intro trouble with their behavior or are unable to perform for some period of time.

If you are committed to either the rent on a venue, or to a performance agreement with a booking agent for a venue or a promoter (for the bigger events), then you could be in a position to either still have to pay the rent or pay a cancellation fee to the venue or promoter if the band is unable to perform for some reason. If the amount of the repayment or cancellation fee is large enough, the band can end up with serious financial problems in the event of a large block of cancellations and no insurance coverage.

Advertising

Another expense related to touring involves advertising. You cannot book dates on a tour and do nothing other than just show up for each show. At a minimum, you will need to have flyers and posters for placement in the cities along the tour route. You will also have to make arrangements to get these materials distributed, which may involve either hiring some individuals on your own in each city to serve as a street team to pass out flyers and put up posters, or hiring a promotions company. Either way, there are costs to the band associated with these activities. If you are promoting your own tour, you may have to purchase media advertising, such as radio spots and print ads. This is another cost to you. Of course, if you are dealing with promoters for all of your shows, the promoter will cover all of the costs of the show, and these issues will not be as important to you.

FOREIGN TOURS

If you stick with your music career and it progresses, you may get the opportunity to perform outside the United States. Before you just pack your bags and equipment and head off, be sure that you have investigated the legal requirements of the foreign country to which you will be going. Most foreign travel requires a passport. You will need to apply for this document well in advance of your trip so that you are sure that you have allowed enough time for your application to be processed and the passport returned to you. You will also need to know if any of the countries you are visiting require you to have a visa. This varies from country to country, and the rules and regulations can change, so it is important to have up-to-date information. The best place to start your investigation is with the travel agent who books your travel arrangements.

Even if you are simply performing in a show and then leaving, many countries will require you to have a work permit before you can perform as a musician. Be sure to start this application process early as well. Work permits are issued by the countries into which you are going, and it can take some time to get all your paperwork in order.

TOURING LIABILITY ISSUES

Because of the liability exposure that results from touring, many of the established bands and bands with record deals set up a separate band business to deal with touring. Then, all of the tour-related contracts are handled through the touring company, and this helps to protect the main band business from liability. This strategy will only help the band if the new touring company is either a corporation, a *limited liability company* (called an LLC), or a *limited liability partnership* (LLP). If you just set up a new assumed name or new partnership, the individual band members still have personal liability exposure. Simply setting up a new venture and calling it something else does not accomplish anything. Before you decide to create a new corporation, you should discuss the situation with your attorney and your tax advisor. (If you do not understand the purpose of this strategy or how to accomplish setting up the new entity, review Chapter 1.)

PROMOTING FOR YOUR SHOWS

As a young band starting out on the local scene, it is up to you to promote for your shows. That means you will need to have flyers and posters, and you will need to be on the scene passing them out two weeks before each show. Always be sure to observe the basic rules of promotion. First, don't put flyers up in a business without asking for permission first. This is true even in the venue where you will be playing your show. Don't put flyers for a show in one club up in another club; it's also better if you don't stand just outside the doors of other clubs passing out flyers for shows in other local venues. You want to promote yourself and your band as professionals, so act like a professional. Don't go to other venues in the immediate area on show night and try to recruit fans to come to your show.

When you are out on the local scene, don't just hang out with the people you already know. Meet new ones—every person you meet is a potential new fan. If people are not coming to your show, take a realistic look at the situation. Are your promotional efforts falling short or is your material just not good enough?

The same general rules apply to promoting for out-of-town shows, except that you will not be spending as much time on the local scene. So you will need to recruit street team members to help you promote by passing out flyers and putting up posters. You will also need to think creatively about ways to promote. Can you pay a pizza delivery place to put your flyers on the top of each box? Are there local businesses who are willing to put your flyers on the counter? If it is a big show, consider paying for an ad either on the radio or in the local paper. Check to see if that city has a paper devoted to the music scene and, if so, advertise there.

Especially as you get to the point of touring, look at the branding of your band. Decide what you want your band to be known for. Is it your stage show, your antics on stage, your material, or your image? Find your niche, and focus on developing it and promoting toward it.

 Musical Note

When you are playing out of town, be sure to get your posters and flyers to the club well in advance of the show so the venue can promote the show. If you have a press pack, send one along.

As you establish a following, you may begin to dream about going on tour with a national act. But you must keep in mind that bands do not get into those slots just because they or their manager have connections with the industry. Many of those tours require the support bands to buy onto the tour, and you may not be able to get on until you have a record deal with a label that can put the money into it.

chapter nine:
The Basics of Copyright

A *copyright* is the legal process by which the creator of an original literary or artistic work is granted the exclusive right to use and exploit that work. The first criteria you have to meet in order to get a copyright is that the work must be *original*. There have been many court cases over what it means to for a work to be original. A detailed analysis of the finer points of this area of the law is beyond the scope of this book. For our purposes, the simplified definition is that an original work cannot be copied exactly from another work. One song may remind people of other songs without violating the copyrights of those songs, but it cannot be the same song, with the same notes, in the same order.

The copyright law sets out the exclusive rights given to the copyright owner. These rights give the owner of the copyright the exclusive rights to do and to authorize any of the following.

- Reproduce the copyrighted work in copies or phonorecords.
- Prepare derivative works based on the copyrighted work.

- Distributed copies or phonorecords of the copyrighted work to the public by sale or other transfers (rental, leasing, or lending) of ownership.
- Perform the copyrighted work publicly.
- Display the copyrighted work publicly.
- Perform the copyrighted work publicly by means of a digital audio transmission (in the case of sound recordings).

The copyright owner gets copyright protection when the work is *created*. The statute defines created as being when the work is fixed in a *copy*. For purposes of this law, copy means a "material object from which the work can be perceived, reproduced, or communicated, either directly or with the aid of a machine."

Musical Note

The law defines a "phonorecord" as a material object in which sounds other than those accompanying a motion picture are fixed, and from which sounds can be perceived, reproduced, or otherwise communicated (for example, a CD).

Basically, what all of this means is that you get copyright protection when your work is put into some kind of physical form. If you come up with a song, that alone does not create a copyright, even though it is your original song. You do not get copyright protection until it becomes a material object. This means you either have to write it down or record it. Once that has happened, you have become the owner of the copyright.

Now that you are the owner, you are generally the only one with exclusive rights to the song. As previously mentioned, each of those rights are different. You should understand what each one gives you.

The first item on the list of exclusive rights is the right to reproduce and record the song. This means you can keep other people from recording your song, and you are the only one who can authorize someone else to record it or use it in any way. This right only lasts until you exploit it for the first time. Once you let anyone record the song, a *compulsory license* is created, which is covered in more detail later.

Item two on the list relates to the creation of *derivative works* based on the copyrighted material. Derivative works are based on one or more preexisting works, and generally include things like arrangements, translations, and sound recordings. For example, if you write a song about your father, and someone comes along and wants to take the words you used to describe your father and add a stanza or two about his or her own father, the new song would be considered based on your song—meaning you could keep the other songwriter from using your work.

The third item is fairly self-explanatory. You have the right to sell recordings of your work to the public.

You will notice that none of the first three exclusive rights mentions anything to do with public versus private use. This is because you hold these exclusive rights, and any use that violates one of these provisions is a violation regardless of the use of the prohibited work. However, the rest of the rights on the list are different. They specifically deal with public use of your work.

The exclusive right to perform your work in public is given to you in item four on the list. The only way anyone else can perform your copyrighted work in public is if you give them permission to do so. You can handle the administrative work of granting that permission yourself. If you choose to go this route, you will be responsible for keeping up with all of the uses that are made of your song and making sure that you get paid for them. This can be a time-consuming process if your song is popular and a lot of people want to perform it.

Instead, most people use one of the performing rights societies—ASCAP, BMI, and SESAC—to handle the administrative work. (see Chapter 8.) Once you decide you are willing to relinquish your exclusive right to perform your work, you can register your song with one of the societies, and it will take care of the paperwork necessary to authorize others to use your song, collect your royalty payments, and distribute your money to you. Of course, you must still meet the membership requirements of the society you choose.

Item number five on the list of exclusive rights does not really apply to music by itself, because you do not display it. However, if your band creates a music video, the music video is also protected by copyright, and the exclusive right to display the video comes into play.

The final item on the list, digital audio transmission, was added to the *Copyright Act* to address the issues that had been created by the Internet. Until the copyright law was changed, the copyright owner had no control over the digital transmission of his or her music. This was basically a case of technology getting ahead of the law. Now the copyright owner has a copyright interest in uses of his or her song when it is digitally transmitted, for instance, by way of a webcast on an Internet radio station.

Of course, as with most areas of the law, there are exceptions to the rules about exclusive rights. Not all of them really apply to musicians and the situations they normally encounter, so only those exceptions that you are likely to encounter are discussed.

The first exception is one called the *fair use doctrine*. This rule says that there is no copyright violation if someone uses your material as part of some other purpose, such as criticism, comment, or news reporting. So the music critic's review of your new album will generally not violate your copyright, even if some of your lyrics are included in the review. The fair use doctrine also covers uses for teaching, scholarship, or research. A music teacher may be able to play part of your song to a class studying music.

In addition to the purpose of the use, the factors that go into determining whether something is a fair use of your protected work are the extent of the portion of your copyrighted work that was used and the effect on the potential market for your work or its value. For example, quoting a line or two of your song in a news report will not violate your copyright. However, if all the words and music to your song is included in with the reviewer's article, your authorization would probably be needed.

If the person wanting to use your copyrighted work is doing so for noncommercial purposes, he or she may be allowed to use more of the work than otherwise allowed under the fair use doctrine. For example, libraries and archives are given an exemption from the copyright rules in order to make copies of your works under the limited circumstances of preserving the work or for some other similar noncommercial use. Likewise, performances at schools or in the course of services in houses of worship are generally allowed, so long as the use is not commercial, there is no charge for admission, and the performers do not get paid.

Your use sometimes creates situations in which you will have to grant a license for others to use your material. This is called a *compulsory license*. There is a process by which the compulsory license is granted when the person who wants to use your material for one of these compulsory purposes—cable television rebroadcasts, PBS, jukeboxes, and digital downloading—gives you a *Notice of Intent to Use*.

If you use part of someone else's work to make fun of it by using either satire or parody, then you can use the copyrighted work without violating the copyright. The standard that courts use in deciding whether a work is a satire or parody, or whether it is a copyright violation, is the purpose for which the work is used. If the court decides that it is, in fact, a satire or parody, then that is considered a fair use of the copyrighted work.

SAMPLING

Sampling, first made popular in the rap genre, involves making an exact digital copy of some portion of another person's recording. It may be something as short as a brief drum sound or an entire guitar track. Either way, copyright issues are involved in this process. If you just stick part of someone else's song in your song, you are violating the original song creator's copyright. Before you record a song that has any samples in it, you must get a license from the copyright owner of the recording and another from the copyright owner of the song itself.

If you try to get around this problem by just playing the part of someone else's song that you want to use and not using their recording of the material, it may keep you from dealing with the recording copyright holder, but you still have to deal with the copyright owner of the song. This is because the copyright to a recording and to the song are not the same thing and are not necessarily held by the same person.

If you create the song and do the recording and producing of the recording yourself, then you own the copyright for both the song and the recording. However, if you write the song, someone else records it, and a third person produces the recording, there are three different sets of rights attached to the song. You have the copyright on the song. The person or entity that performed on the recording owns the rights to the performance. The producer owns the copyright for the particular version of the song that was recorded (the master).

Musical Note

If you are dealing with a record label, they may expect you to have all of the clearances you need to include the sample in your recording.

Getting permission to sample can be difficult since you may be dealing with different people and their record labels. To get permission, you will have to track down the appropriate person or entity, tell them what you want to use, and negotiate a fee for the use. This is an area in which you may want to have the help of an attorney. There is no set fee for the sampling rights—it just comes down to a negotiation between the parties involved.

ALBUM ART

As a young band, you will probably be designing your own album covers for your first recordings. When you do so, you must remember that all of the artwork on the album has copyright protection, and the owner of the copyright is not the band. Unless it can be classified as a *work for hire* (discussed on p. 88), the particular individual who created the artwork owns the copyright. Additionally, you cannot use work done by others on your album unless you have their authorization. It is not uncommon for bands without professional assistance to take photos and designs they have seen other places and use them on the album. When you do this, you are probably violating someone's copyright. Have you seen a really neat photo in a magazine and decided to use it on your album cover? You have then violated the photographer's copyright, and depending on the particular facts, maybe the magazine's as well. (See Chapter 11 for more issues relating to album covers.)

COAUTHORS

If the copyrighted work was created by more than one person, they each have a copyright interest in the work. Each one has the right to use and exploit the work that has been created, but they cannot exclude the other copyright owners from using it. When one of the copyright owners makes use of the copyrighted work, he or she must account to the other owners for any money made from the use and for any damage to the value of the copyright.

WORKS FOR HIRE

The basic copyright rules state that the person who creates a work owns the copyright. The big exception to this rule involves *work for hire*. There are two ways a work can end up being classified as a work for hire.

The first method involves the traditional employer/ employee situation. For example, assume that Writer Bob is a professional songwriter with a large stable of artists for whom he writes. Bob's business is strong, and he is too busy to write enough material for his clients, so he hires Sam to work for him. Sam works as Bob's employee, writing songs or parts of songs under Bob's direction. In this instance, Bob is the owner of the copyright and Sam, because he is Bob's employee, has no copyright interest in the songs he writes for Bob's clients.

The second way a work for hire can be created is if it qualifies as a specially commissioned work. For example, your band has just finished its first CD, and because you are new and do not have a record deal, you have done the recording yourself. You need some kind of design for the album cover, but unfortunately, no one in your band has any graphic design or art skills. However, your drummer's cousin does. When the band hires the cousin to design the album cover, the work can be considered a work for hire because it was specifically commissioned for the album. In order for the band to own the copyright under the work for hire rules, the band must have a written agreement with the cousin for the album art, and the agreement must specifically state that the art is a work for hire.

DURATION OF THE COPYRIGHT

Your copyright protection lasts for the duration of your lifetime, plus seventy years. If the copyright is owned by more than one person, then the period is seventy years from the death of the last surviving author. In a work for hire, the copyright period is ninety-five years after publication or 120 years after creation, whichever occurs first.

Once the copyright protection period ends, the work is in the *public domain*. This means that anyone is free to use the work without having to pay for the usage right. If you are using something that you think is in the public domain, you should consult an attorney to be sure of the status. There is no one place you can go to determine if a particular work is in the public domain or not—this will require some investigation on your part.

You also need to be mindful about how you use public domain items. For example, the painting of the Mona Lisa is in the public domain. However, if you decide to put a photograph of Mona on your album cover, you cannot forget about the copyright owned by the photographer who took the picture.

REGISTRATION

Your copyright comes into legal existence at the time of creation. It is not necessary for you to register your copyright anywhere in order for the right to come into existence. However, you may still want to take the additional step of formally registering your material with the copyright office. Doing so will help you should you ever have to go to court to sue someone for violating your copyright or to defend yourself if you get sued for violating someone else's. The registration helps you establish the date of your copyright and puts others on notice of its existence.

If you sue someone for violating your copyright and you win, certain damages, such as attorney's fees and *statutory damages*, can only be paid if you have registered. Registration is also important because it allows you protection from the importation of infringing copies of your work. You cannot get this protection from the United States Customs Service without being registered.

How to Register

The registration process is fairly simple and straightforward. You will first need to get a copy of the application form. You may request it by mail from:

Library of Congress
Copyright Office
101 Independence Avenue, S.E.
Washington, DC 20559-6000

You can also call the forms hotline at 202-707-9100 or get the forms online at **www.copyright.gov/forms**. Which form you need depends on what it is you are registering. Sound recordings (copyrighting the performance of the song) need Form SR. To copyright the music and lyrics, you should use Form PA. For visual arts (such as movies and DVDs), use Form VA.

The completed form, along with the application fee (presently $30) and the required number of copies of the work, should be sent to the address above. Check the forms and instructions for the number of copies you need. You will not get back the copies you send to the copyright office. The copies must be either a printed copy or a copy of the recording itself. If you have properly submitted everything, you should receive your copyright registration in about four to five months. Be sure the copyright office gets your new address if you move after you file the application but before you receive your registration back.

 Musical Note

Additional information regarding copyright registration is available on the official Copyright Office website, **www.copyright.gov**.

TRANSFERRING OWNERSHIP OF COPYRIGHTS

Because a copyright involves an ownership right, it can be transferred just like any other piece of property. A copyright owner can assign or sell the copyright to someone else (done by using a written contract) or can exclusively license the copyright. The transfer must be done in writing and be signed by the owner of the copyright. The owner should sign the transfer documents before a notary public.

Once the paperwork has been signed, the transfer should be recorded with the Copyright Office. There is a fee for recording the transfer.

Copyright transfers often occur in music publishing. However, before you transfer your copyright to anyone, you should be absolutely certain you are making a good deal. When you sell your house, you cannot just change your mind and get it back. The same is true with copyright transfers. This transfer cannot just be undone if you have made a bad deal with a music publisher or other entity.

TERMINATION OF THE TRANSFER

Congress has passed laws that allow the person who created a work and transferred the copyright to terminate the transfer. There is a limited window of time, however, during which this termination can be done. If the work was created after 1978, you have a period of five years that begins at the end of thirty-five years after the date of execution of the grant. If the grant covers a right of publication, it starts thirty-five years from the date of publication of the work or at the end of forty years from the signing of the transfer agreement, whichever is earliest. For works created prior to 1978, the termination period is five years beginning fifty-six years after the date of registration of the copyright.

The termination is done by written notice, which must be served on the new holders of the copyright and must state the effective date of the termination. This effective date must fall within the five year window previously discussed. Since the statute says the notice must comply with the rules and regulations established by the Copyright Office, you should be sure to check with them when you wish to terminate to determine what regulations are in effect at that time.

INTERNATIONAL COPYRIGHT ISSUES

The rules and regulations previously discussed apply to works created in the United States. The protections offered by our laws only protect your work against violations in the United States. Each country passes its own laws on how to protect the rights of someone who creates on original work, and these laws vary widely from country to country. This means that there is no one international copyright office, and there is no automatic international copyright protection.

There are two major international treaties that affect copyrights—the *Berne Union for Protection of Literary and Artistic Property* and the *Universal Copyright Convention*. The status of your copyright protection depends not just on the laws passed by each country, but also on whether the country in question is a *signatory* to one or both of these treaties. Being a signatory means the country has signed the treaty and the government of that country has ratified the treaty in accordance with their laws.

In the countries that have signed the treaties, your copyright protection will be very similar to what you get in the United States. However, there are countries that have neither signed one of the treaties nor passed any laws themselves creating copyrights. In those countries, your work has no copyright protection at all, regardless of its status in the United States.

INFRINGEMENT

When a person violates someone's copyright, they are guilty of *infringement*. You can be in trouble for copyright infringement even if you did not violate the copyright intentionally. The person claiming the copyright infringement must prove that he or she owned the copyright and that you copied his or her work without permission. If you are found to have infringed on a copyright, you can either be ordered by the judge to destroy all the copies of your work or be required to pay money damages to the copyright holder.

The money damages would be based on how much money you have improperly made. You can also be required to pay the copyright owner's attorney's fees and court costs. If the judge rules that you *willfully infringed* on a copyright (in other words, you knew you were violating a copyright and went ahead and did it anyway), you could even be facing criminal prosecution and jail time for the copyright infringement.

Copyright infringement cases are complex and you should never try to represent yourself, either as the copyright owner or as the one accused of the infringement. If you think that someone has infringed on a copyright you own, you should consult an attorney to discuss your options. When looking for a lawyer, find one who specializes in intellectual property.

chapter ten:

The Business of Publishing

Music publishing is the process by which the copyright holder *exploits* the work. A work, such as a song, is exploited when it is offered for commercial use. If a song you wrote gets selected to be part of the soundtrack of a movie, the movie producer must license your song in order to use it. The licensing process is called *publishing*. The term publishing encompasses activities like finding people who are willing to pay you for the right to use your song, handling the administrative part of actually issuing the license, and managing the financial issues so that you actually get paid for each use of your work.

DEFINITIONS

Before getting into the business of publishing, you need to have an understanding of the meaning of some basic terms.

- The *license* is the agreement that sets out the terms under which the owner of a song grants another person or entity the right to use the song in some way.
- A *mechanical license* is used when a copyright owner is giving another person the right to make an audio recording of the song.

- A *synchronization license* (also commonly referred to as a *synch license*) is required when the song will be used with accompanying video, such as in a movie, television show, or music video.
- A *master use license* is the license that allows you to take a recording and reproduce it. The recording is called a *master*.
- The *statutory rate* is the royalty amount, set by law, that the copyright owner gets paid for a mechanical license. This rate is subject to change, but right now it is 8.5¢ per song and 1.65¢ per minute. The parties to a United Sates license agreement are free to negotiate a different rate; however, even when they do so the statutory rate is the benchmark. For rights in mechanical licenses in other countries, the mechanical license rates are set by law and administered by government mechanical licensing agencies.
- A *compulsory license* is a license created by the *Copyright Act* and occurs once a copyright owner has publicly distributed phonorecords of a musical work. When that happens, any person wishing to record that work must give the copyright holder notice that his or her other work is being used. This must be done within thirty days before the making of the recording and prior to the distribution of any of the recordings. Proceeding under the compulsory license provisions requires the user to pay the copyright owner the statutory mechanical license fee and provide the owner with a monthly accounting.
- To *exploit* a song means to use it for commercial purposes.
- A *print license* is the license that allows your song to be used in written form, such as sheet music or in a concert arrangement. This is the first type of music

license to be used. Because the music was being printed and distributed, much like books are printed and distributed in a process called publishing, the license of music for printed use came to be called *music publishing*.

 Musical Note

In actual practice, not that many people get a license to use a copyrighted song by using the compulsory license law—they just contact the copyright owner and directly negotiate a mechanical license.

DECIDING WHETHER YOU NEED PROFESSIONAL PUBLISHING HELP

If you are a songwriter, it is technically possible for you to handle all of your own publishing duties. If you choose to go this route, you will have to file all of your own copyright paperwork, locate artists willing to record your song, negotiate the license agreement, and then do all of the accounting and auditing work to be sure you have received all of your money. If you are a musician in a band, and the only use you plan on making of your song is to record it on a CD with your band, this may be a relatively easy task. You will need to register your copyright, license your song to your band, and join one of the performance rights societies, but the other administrative tasks will not be a problem for you.

Of course, this also means there is no one working for you to get your song placed in a commercial, television show, or movie. Therefore, unless your band's CD sells extremely well, you will not be making much money from your song. As a brand new songwriter writing for a brand new band, this is likely to be the situation anyway, so you may not be missing out on any substantial funding. If you have a good management team working for you, your manager may be able to find some of these commercial opportunities for your band, but you will be missing out on the network of connections that a good music publisher has created.

However, before you rush out and sign a publishing contract, you need to remember that there is a very large downside to the standard publishing arrangement. Your publisher will be asking you to give up ownership of your copyright by transferring it to him or her. In exchange, the standard publishing contract will give you 50% of the monies received from the exploitation of your song. As you may recall from the previous chapter, transferring your ownership of the copyright is basically a permanent deal. If, six months into your contract with the publisher, you decide that you are not happy with the way they have handled your song, there is nothing you can do to force them to transfer the ownership of your copyright back to you. They own it now, and they can make you wait until the termination of transfer period comes around—which, as you recall, is at least thirty-five years away—to get the copyright back.

Administrative Agreements

As your songwriting career begins to reach the next level, and artists and producers are using your songs, the administrative parts of publishing may become too time consuming for you to keep handling. At this point in your career, you may want to consider an alternative to the publishing contract. It is called an *administration agreement*. In this arrangement, the company provides the administrative and clerical services for you, such as issuing the licenses and collecting the money, but you maintain the ownership of your copyright. The administrator will generally make between 10% and 25% of the gross monies received from the exploitation of the song. Instead of basically being a permanent deal like the publishing contract, administration agreements are for a specific time period. Once the contract period is complete, the deal between the two parties is basically over.

Forming Your Own Publishing Company

If you decide to handle the publishing yourself, you should consider formally establishing yourself as a publishing company. You will have to do so if you plan on performing publishing functions on any songs you did not write. When you are ready to publish your material, your first step needs to be to pick a name for your publishing company and submit it for approval to the performance rights society with which you will be affiliated. When you join one of the societies as a writer-member, you cannot have the same name as any other society member. The same thing is true of your publishing company. The society will not allow you to use a name if it is the same as or too close to the name of another publisher. You may also want to check with your state corporations section and your local county clerk to see if the name you have picked is also available as a corporate name or as an assumed name. (see Chapter 2.)

One you have permission to use the name, you need to establish your formal business structure. You will need to decide whether you will operate as a sole proprietorship or as a corporation. If you are a sole proprietor and are calling your publishing business by any name other than your own legal name, you will need to file an *assumed name certificate* (sometimes called a *fictitious name certificate* or a d/b/a—shorthand for *doing business as*). This certificate is filed with the county clerk in the county where your business is located.

If you decide to incorporate and did not check with your state's records prior to selecting your name, it is possible that the name approved by the performance rights society might not be available for you to use as a corporate name. If you find yourself in that situation, just select whatever name you want to use for your corporation. It does not matter if the performing rights society will approve your corporate name or not. You will still be operating your publishing business under the name approved by the performance rights society. Once you have received your corporate charter back from your state, then you file a corporate assumed name certificate showing that the corporation is doing business as the name approved by the society. You will file the assumed name certificate in both the county where your business is located and then with the state corporation section.

Example:

You want to name your publishing company Susan's Publishing, and you have decided to affiliate with ASCAP. When you submit the Susan's Publishing name to ASCAP, they tell you that you cannot use it. So, you change to Bubba's Records, which ASCAP approves. When you start your incorporation process, your state tells you that you cannot use Bubba's Records. At that point, you decide you will incorporate as Susan and Bubba, Inc., and your state approves this name. You then go to your local county clerk's office and fill out the assumed name certificate, stating that Susan and Bubba, Inc. is doing business as Bubba's Records. Then you do all of your publishing work under the Bubba's Records name.

For more information about selecting a form for your business and setting up the business, see Chapter 1. All of the material on selecting a form of business and getting started with it apply to all businesses—whether they are bands engaged in musical careers, songwriters operating a publishing company, or mechanics starting a repair shop business.

If you plan on doing publishing work for other artists, you will need to create a second company and affiliate with the other primary performance rights society. If you sign up with ASCAP, for example, as Bubba's Records, you will need to register a second company with BMI. The reason the second company is needed is that both artists and publishers can only be affiliated with one or the other at any time. If you belong to ASCAP, you cannot affiliate with BMI until you quit ASCAP or affiliate a second, distinct company with BMI.

Your publishing operations will have to be able to work with both companies because the societies require the publisher and writers on any one song to be affiliated with the same company. In other words, an ASCAP writer cannot have a BMI publisher and vice-versa. Since separate companies are separate legal entities, one company can join ASCAP and the other company can join BMI, and you can work with the artists from either society. This does not mean that an ASCAP writer and a BMI writer cannot collaborate and write a song together. When this happens, ASCAP collects the money for the ASCAP writer and BMI collects the money for the BMI writer. The ASCAP writer still has to have an ASCAP publisher and the BMI writer has to have a BMI publisher.

WHAT TO LOOK FOR WHEN SELECTING A PUBLISHER

Once your songwriting career has reached the point where it makes sense for you to hire a publishing company, you have to decide which one to use. As in just about any industry, there are very large firms, one-person operations, and everything in-between. There are advantages and disadvantages to each.

The very large firms have sophisticated operations with large staffs. They may be owned by a record label, film studio, or production company. Their size enables them to have personnel who specialize in placing your songs in the various money-making areas. They have separate departments to manage the copyrights and the licensing operations, a legal staff to help it all go smoothly, and a sizeable accounting department to keep up with the financial dealings related to each of your songs. Because of the number of deals they do and the other businesses they sometimes operate, they have vast experience in dealing with the issues related to placing your song for commercial exploitation.

In order to sustain all of these employees, though, the publishing firm will own and be responsible for managing thousands of songs. If you are now a well-known writer and your material is making a lot of money for the publisher, then the number of other songs will not hurt your ability to make money. If you are not fortunate enough to have reached this level yet, the size of the publisher may work to your disadvantage. While the big firms have tremendous contacts and networks in place, your song may be so far off the radar that none of these great contacts do you any good financially.

If you go with a smaller operation, your material is much less likely to get lost in the shuffle. Because of the limited number of other songs owned by the small publisher, your song should get plenty of attention. Unfortunately, all of the attention in the world will not get your song into the right hands. If you transfer your copyright to a publisher who lacks the ability, either because they do not know what they are doing or they do not have the contacts they need to exploit your song, then you are never going to see any significant financial success as a result of the song you have written.

You should not, however, let these things keep you from ever dealing with a small publisher. Some small operations are just as successful for their clients as the big firms. The key for you is to do your homework and check out any publisher with whom you are considering doing business. Ask what kind of success they have had getting their clients' songs in movies, television, commercials, or even Broadway shows.

In choosing a publisher, you might also consider smaller publishers who have copublishing agreements with a larger publishing firm. Depending on how the arrangement is structured, this may give you the benefit of both the attention you receive from a small operation and the size and connection advantages you get with a big firm. Copublishing just means there is more than one entity that owns the publishing rights to a particular song. The agreement between the copublishers will determine which company handles the administration of the rights, and how the other rights and obligations are divided.

CONTRACT ISSUES

The *songwriter agreement* is the contract between the songwriter and the publishing company. There are two main kinds of songwriter agreements. One is the *single song contract*, which is just what it sounds like. It is a contract that governs the publishing of one song written by the songwriter. The other is the *exclusive songwriter's agreement*, in which the songwriter agrees to write songs only for the publisher during a given period of time. This period of time will likely be at least one year but should not exceed seven years, including option years. As with other types of contracts in the entertainment industry, the seven-year period is the standard maximum because the laws in some states set seven as the legal maximum.

The songwriter's contract has many provisions in it that are similar to the provisions contained in recording contracts, so you may want to also review the chapter on recording for help in understanding these terms. The publishing contract may or may not be tied to a recording contract. If it is tied to a recording contract, the publishing contract will transfer ownership of the copyrights for all the songs on a particular album to the publisher, and the term of the songwriter's obligation to write songs for the publisher will be the same as the recording contract term. When the term of one ends, then both contracts terminate.

There are some contract provisions that will be found in both the single song contract and the exclusive songwriter's contract. The big provision in the contract is the one that provides for the sale of the song from the writer to the publisher.

The contract will also contain provisions giving the publisher the licensing rights in several different areas. The publisher will get the right to license the performances of the song— this right will then usually be assigned to one of the performance societies. Additional licensing rights will be granted for recordings, Internet downloads, movies, television, commercials, theatrical productions, and for any other future uses that may be developed.

Another important section of the contract deals with the compensation to be paid to the songwriter. How much the writer is paid depends on what usage is covered by the license. For performance licenses, the writer is generally paid directly by the performance rights society and will not receive any additional compensation under the publishing agreement. For print licenses, such as for sheet music, writer's contracts usually provide for payment of some number of cents per copy of sheet music sold. This number is generally between five and ten cents. For folios (books containing printed music for several songs), the writer will either get a percentage of the wholesale price (in the neighborhood of 10%) or the proceeds received from the printer of the folio will be split evenly between the writer and the publisher.

The fifty/fifty split is the general rule for the other licenses, such as the mechanical license for audio recording, the synchronization license for video use, as well as for the money received from the exploitation of the work in foreign countries. The publisher will have an agreement with local publishers in other countries to manage the foreign uses of your work, so your split in your contract with the publishing company will be fifty percent of what the publishing company receives from the foreign publisher.

Accounting Provisions

Your contract should contain provisions outlining a schedule for when your publisher will pay royalty fees to you. You also want the publisher to be contractually bound to provide you with an accounting of all the monies that have been paid in relation to your song. When you are reviewing the contract, you also want to look carefully for any language that charges costs against your royalty payment. In a typical record deal, there are all kinds of items that come out of your royalty money before you see any of it.

Publishing is different—the only thing that should be deducted from your royalty payments are costs to collect your money, such as payments owed to the Harry Fox Agency, and any sub-publishing fees for foreign exploitation of your song. (A discussion of what the *Harry Fox Agency* is and why you would be paying them money occurs later in this chapter.) There may also be a provision that deducts some or all of the costs of any demo recording paid for by the publisher and used to market your material to potential users.

Licensing Provisions

If your publisher is affiliated with your record label, there is one provision that you should always get included in the publishing contract. This provision states that the publisher cannot license your music to its affiliated record label on terms that are less favorable to you than the industry standards.

As the creator of a song, you may not want your publisher to have complete, unfettered control over how your song is used and for what purposes it is licensed. If this is your position, then request a clause in the contract that requires the publisher to get your permission before agreeing to license your song.

Revision Provisions

Another issue that can arise in a publishing arrangement is the song that is under a publishing agreement but never gets exploited by the publishing company. If that happens, your song is just stuck in the clutches of the publishing company (and most likely owned by them), but you are not making any money from it. To avoid this problem, you can request that a reversion provision be included in your publishing contract. A reversion clause says that, if the publishing company does not exploit your song within a specified time period, then ownership of the copyright of that song returns to you.

Exclusive Songwriter Contract Provisions

There are some contract provisions that are found in exclusive songwriter contracts, but not in single song contracts. Because the writer in the exclusive songwriter deal is contractually limited to writing songs just for the publisher, the writer needs to be able to financially support him- or herself during the term of the agreement. One way this can be done is through the payment of advances to the writer. If you are getting an advance, the contract will contain the amount of the advance and how it will be paid. An advance can be paid all at once at the beginning of the contract term or in several installments (for instance, either quarterly or monthly). If you have gotten an advance, then the contract will contain a recoupment clause so that the publishing company gets its advance money back.

The publisher will generally be able to recoup its money from your royalties before you see any of the money, except for performance royalties. The performing rights societies handle the task of dividing the money between the writer and the publisher. The writer's share gets paid directly to the writer; so, the publisher does not have an opportunity to recoup any advance money out of your performance rights payment.

Most exclusive songwriter contracts will contain a minimum delivery clause. The purpose of this clause is to ensure, from the publisher's point of view, that the songwriter does not spend the term of the contract collecting an advance but not producing any songs. Therefore, the contract will contain a number of songs that the writer is required to provide to the publisher during the contract period.

The publisher will also want to have included in the contract a clause of some sort that helps protect them from poor quality songs. One way is to have the delivery requirement be stated in such a way that only songs that are included on an album count toward the minimum. Another method is for the publisher to have the right to reject songs as part of the delivery requirement if the publisher believes that the songs submitted are not good enough. Of course, if you are the writer, giving the publisher this right gives them a fair amount of discretion in determining whether or not you have satisfied the minimum delivery clause.

If you are working with another writer, you want to be sure that your contract gives you credit for those songs written with a collaborator in your minimum delivery count. Your credit may be equal to your interest in the song. For instance, if there are three writers and you each own ⅓ of the song, you would be credited with ⅓ of a song toward your minimum.

HARRY FOX AGENCY

At this point, you may be wondering who Harry Fox is and why you might owe him money out of your publishing royalties. The *Harry Fox Agency* (HFA) is a company that represents music publishing companies, and the services they provide include the issuance of mechanical and digital licenses, the collection and distribution of royalties, and the performance of royalty audits. They previously issued synchronization licenses, but have discontinued this service.

Especially if you have signed a contract with a publishing company, it may seem like you are paying both the publisher and Harry Fox to do the same things for you, and you may not want your publisher to sign on with HFA. But there are good reasons HFA represents some of the largest publishing companies in the country. One main reason is that, periodically, HFA audits the books of record companies. All of HFA's clients benefit from the audit, which is done at no additional cost to the publisher. Any monies recovered from the audit are distributed among the agency's clients. Record company audits are very expensive, and using HFA allows publishers the benefit of an audit, which only the largest of them could ever afford to do on their own. This alone makes the commission charged by HFA worth the cost.

The Harry Fox Agency does not represent writers, only publishers. If you are a writer and are going to be setting up your own publishing company, you will want to consider retaining HFA, so you will need to check with them to see about their current requirements.

The Harry Fox Agency works on a commission, which means they receive a percentage of your royalty income from the licenses they issue. The commission percentage is presently 6.75%, but this number does change. You can contact them at:

Harry Fox Agency
711 Third Avenue
New York, N.Y. 10017
212-370-5330
www.harryfox.com

DIGITAL DOWNLOADS

The payment of digital royalties begins with registration with *Sound Exchange.* (see Chapter 8.) From the songwriter's perspective, digital downloads are dealt with by using a regular mechanical license. Sound Exchange deals with the royalty rights belonging to the copyright holder of the sound recording.

Remember that, with a sound recording, there are two copyrights involved. One copyright belongs to the musical work (the writer of the song and his or her publishing company) and the other to the owner of the recording itself. Sound Exchange, therefore, deals with the record company, recording producer, and the recording artist and does not collect royalty payments for writers for use of the musical work. These payments come under the regular mechanical license.

FOREIGN PUBLISHING

Because of the way international laws work, your publishing company based in the United States can issue licenses for uses of your work in the United States. If you are going to make money from the exploitation of your song in foreign countries, you have to deal with publishing companies who operate in each country in which your work will be used. This foreign company is called a *sub-publisher*. If you decide to set up your own publishing company, you will have to investigate foreign music publishing companies and enter into contracts with them yourself in order to protect your foreign royalty rights. An advantage to dealing with a publishing company is that they already have these agreements in place.

The foreign sub-publisher has to be paid for its services, which is done on a percentage basis. Your contract with your publishing company will deal with that by paying you the royalty percentage based on the funds they receive from the sub-publisher.

Example:

Assume you have written a song that is going to be used in a recording to be made in Germany. Your publishing company in the United States cannot issue the mechanical license for this recording, so they have to enter into a contract with a publishing company in

Germany and have the German company issue the license. The two companies agree to split the license royalty on the German recording equally. If the mechanical license generates $100,000 in income, the German publisher receives $50,000. Your publishing company gets the other $50,000 and pays your royalty percentage. If your royalty percentage is 50%, then you would make $25,000.

Royalties on performances in foreign countries work the same way. The performance rights societies in the U.S. (ASCAP, BMI, and SESAC) monitor and collect royalties on performances in the United States. Royalties on foreign performances are collected by performance rights organizations in the individual countries. The publisher's share of the royalty is paid to the foreign sub-publisher, who in turn pays your U.S. publisher. The writer's share of the money is paid to your U.S. performance rights society and they pay that money directly to you, not to the publisher. Most of the performance rights organizations in foreign countries are owned and administered by the governments of those countries.

KARAOKE

It seems hard to imagine that there might be significant legal issues involved in karaoke night at your local bar—but they do exist. The songs on the karaoke machine are almost all protected by copyrights. When the copyrighted song is performed in the bar, the owner of the copyright is owed a performance royalty. The general rule that the venue is responsible for obtaining a performance license from ASCAP, BMI, and SESAC should apply to karaoke bars as well, but not all bars have seen it that way. At the time of the writing of this book, ASCAP has filed lawsuits against a number of karaoke bars in fifteen states, based on the bars' failure to obtain the necessary licenses.

There are also license and royalty issues related to having the song included on the karaoke machine in the first place. For the songwriter and publisher, this is another opportunity to earn a license fee. The manufacturer of the machine has to license the songs from the copyright owner and obtain a print license in order to include a printed version of the song's lyrics with the machine. The writer and publisher will earn a statutory mechanical royalty for having the song included on the machine, which will be paid based on the number of tapes distributed, and a negotiated fee—some number of cents per lyric sheet distributed.

ON BROADWAY

If one of your songs is selected to be part of a Broadway show, there are several ways in which royalties become payable. At the beginning of the process, the show's producers may option your song and pay you an option fee. An *option* is a contract in which you grant a prospective purchaser of some property item you own the right to purchase the property under specific terms and conditions. In the Broadway scenario, the purchasers are buying the exclusive right to use your material at some point in the future. There will be a deadline in the agreement so that, if the deadline comes and goes without the option being exercised, you are free to put your material back on the open market. The money you receive from the option is the amount you are paid to take your material off the market during the option period. If the producers exercise the option, then you will receive more money for the actual use of your material. The producers will often pay you an advance on your royalties.

Once the show begins its run, you will begin to receive royalty payments. A typical Broadway show has three stages—the off-Broadway (generally out-of-town) run that occurs prior to the Broadway opening, the Broadway/New York main run of the show, and then the touring productions. Every time the show is performed, you earn a royalty. You also have additional royalty payments from the cast album and maybe from the movie production if the show is successful. Additionally, other artists will be more likely to cover your song from the show, resulting in additional monies to you.

The actual amounts and structures of your royalty payments are determined by the agreements between you, your publisher, and the producers. You can get some guidance as to what these terms might be by studying the basic union contract for composers and lyricists.

HEADED FOR HOLLYWOOD

There are several ways music is used in movies. It can either be background music or it can be a song that is actually sung in the movie. Some songs are written specifically for the movie while other movies make use of existing songs, which may or may not have already been popular hits. The song may be sung by the actors in the movie or a recording artist's version of the song may be used.

How much the writer makes for all of this depends on many factors. Unlike the recording of the song, where the license fee is generally tied to the statutory mechanical license fee, the *synchronization license* is a negotiated fee. The synch license is used here because the movie involves the synchronization of the visual images in the movie with the audio of the song. Some of the things that help determine the value of a song in a movie include:

- how it will be used (a small number of bars versus the whole song performed in the movie—primary theme song versus background music);
- whether the song is or has been a big hit;
- how long the license period is;
- whether the producers will guarantee that the song will be included on the movie soundtrack album; and,
- whether the movie will include a recording of the song by a famous artist or not.

This is another instance when the advice and expertise of an experienced publisher can be a tremendous asset. It is the publisher's job to keep up with what the current industry standards are for movie usage and to negotiate the best deal for you. Your financing will also vary if you have been hired by the production company to write the music as work for hire. In that event, you receive your negotiated payment for the work you do, and the copyright and publishing income belong to the production company.

There is also a royalty opportunity when the movie is released on video, DVD, and cable television. Many times, the writer will receive a one-time fee for the video usage, but some songwriters have been able to negotiate a per-video royalty payment.

TELEVISION SERIES AND MOVIES

Music is used in television in much the same way it is in movies—as a theme song, as background music, or as part of the story. For existing songs, the music is licensed by use of a synch license, with the terms negotiated between the publisher and the television show producer. In addition to the fees for use of the song in the series or movie, you can also negotiate compensation for use of the song if the movie or series is rebroadcast onto subscription television or syndicated.

If a songwriter is being hired to compose all the music for a series, then this work will be treated as work for hire. The television producer will own the copyright to the material you write during the contract period.

COMMERCIALS

If your song is being used as part of a commercial to advertise a movie, you probably will not get separate royalties from the use in the commercial, as your synch license with the movie production company probably gives them the right to use your song for this purpose for free. The same thing will be true of songs used in television productions, unless the commercial uses your song as the primary focus of the commercial, in which case you may receive an additional payment.

You can also earn significant publishing income by having your song chosen to be in a commercial advertising a product or service. You will generally receive a one-time fee for the use of your song for a set period of time—for example, $50,000 to use the song for one year.

chapter eleven:
The Business Aspects of Artwork

When you reach the point in your career where you have your first deal with a record label, your involvement in the creation of your album artwork will likely not be that extensive. What input you do have will be determined by the terms of your contract with the label. If you have negotiated the right to be consulted on the artwork, you will have an opportunity to make your feelings known to the label, but they will not be obligated to do things your way.

As your stature rises, so does the degree of influence you have. Once you begin to reach the top levels, you will have the ability to design the album art yourself and the label will have only limited control of the content.

Generally, even when an artist has control of the album art, he or she only has control over the creative side of the art. The label will always have the final say in regard to the business side, because they are concerned about the potential for legal liability. They will, through the legal staff, decide what licenses and copyright issues exist and how those issues should be resolved. If the label believes that anything on your album art violates the law or will otherwise cause the label to be exposed to liability from a lawsuit, they will have the right to make you change it.

Before you have a record deal, however, you will probably be recording and distributing CDs yourself. While this gives you total creative control, you also have the sole responsibility for complying with all the legal requirements without having the advantage of the label's stable of attorneys. It is impossible in a book of this type to have a comprehensive discussion of every kind of issue that might arise, but an understanding of the general issues and the basics is a must. After you have read this chapter and the one on copyrights, any further questions you have about your specific album and its art should be directed to a qualified attorney.

COPYRIGHT ISSUES

There are two sides to how album art is impacted by the copyright laws—the copyright protection that your album art has once it has been created and the copyright protection afforded to artwork created by another person that you want to use on your album. You cannot use someone else's work on your album without obtaining his or her permission (and probably paying them a fee for the use of their work). Even if you design your own artwork and decide you want to use a photograph of the band on the cover, you have to deal with the fact that the photographer has a copyright on the picture. If the photo is one that was taken by a photographer that you hired just for the purpose of taking a picture to use on your album, then you should have the photographer acknowledge—in writing—that the photo was a work for hire and that you (either the individual members of the band as a partnership or the band's corporation) own the copyright.

If the photo was taken by the photographer under any circumstances other than work for hire, the photographer owns the copyright. If you just stick the photo on your album, you have *infringed upon* (violated) the photographer's copyright. In order to use the photo, you must get the rights to use it from the photographer. You do this by negotiating the purchase of one-time rights to use the picture, with the one-time use being on all the album covers for that particular CD.

If the photo is of anything other than the band members, you also have to be aware of possible copyright and privacy issues related to the underlying thing or person being photographed. Some things you take pictures of are not protected by copyright, and you can use these things freely. For instance, if you want to put a picture of a tree on your album, the tree does not have copyrights to itself and it does not have any privacy rights to be protected. On the other hand, if someone has painted a mural on a wall in your neighborhood, and you think a picture of that mural would be perfect for your album cover, you have to deal with the ownership of the mural.

You cannot just hire a photographer to take a picture of it on a work for hire basis and be done. You will have to determine (by asking and checking any available documentation) who owns the rights to the mural. It could be either the painter himself or the owner of the building, depending on the circumstances of under which the mural was painted. In that scenario, you need the rights to use the photo that was taken and the right to commercially exploit the image of the mural.

If your album art contains a picture of a person, then you must have that person's permission to use the photo. This is because everyone has a privacy right and a right to control how their image and likeness are used. If you are planning to use a photograph of anyone on your album, even if it just one of your friends, you have to have them sign a *model release*. This release gives you the right to commercially use your friend's picture. The same thing is true of photographs of celebrities, even if you took the picture yourself. Although celebrities are public figures, you cannot use photographs of them on your album art without their consent.

If you create your own artwork for the album, you own the copyright for the artwork. If you hire a graphic designer to create the album art, you must address the copyright issues in the artwork created. You should set up the agreement with the designer so that it is a work for hire and the fee you pay to the designer gives you all the rights to the work. That way, you can use it for any purpose. If the artist maintains the copyright, you will have to deal with purchasing the rights to use the art for your album.

Liner Notes

If you are creating your own album, you also need to know what needs to be on the album or liner notes somewhere to protect your copyrights. If you are reprinting any of the lyrics to your songs on the liner, you need to have the traditional copyright notice. For example, if your song was written in 2005, then the copyright notice is "©2005."

When you print the lyrics, be sure to identify each song with the composers of both the music and the lyrics. If the writer is affiliated with a performance society, then that affiliation should be included by the writer's name. You need to do the same thing on the CD label itself if it contains a listing of the individual songs with writer identification.

The separate copyright interest in the sound recording must also be addressed on the album cover or liner and on the

CD label itself. The copyright symbol for the sound recording is different from the copyright symbol for the printed lyrics. The sound recording symbol is ℗ instead of ©. If the band has done the recording itself, then the copyright notation would be the sound recording copyright symbol followed by the name of the band. You will also want to include the following statement: "Unauthorized duplication is a violation of the law."

DESIGN ISSUES

When designing your album cover, be sure to put the band's name and the name of the album on the front cover and on the spine. You should also be sure that the same information appears on the CD label itself. Especially for bands trying to break into the business and get a record deal, including the band's website address is also a good idea.

Finding a Graphic Designer on a Budget

If money is no object, you can hire a professional graphic artist to design your album cover. If, on the other hand, you are like most bands financing their own album, you will need to save money wherever you can. If you do not have art talent yourself, you might check with art schools or programs in your area for inexperienced artists who will be less expensive. You might even be fortunate enough to find a student who would do the work just for the experience and exposure. They would probably want the right to use the work in their portfolio, but may not charge you much, if anything.

chapter twelve:
Doing Business with a Record Label

Most bands dream of someday landing a deal with a record label. This chapter covers issues related to your dealings with the label, particularly the terms of the recording contract. Most of this chapter focuses on what you can expect in a contract from a major label. The next chapter focuses on independent, or *indie*, labels.

Before you deal with a label, you need to know as much about the process as possible. However, you should never negotiate your own record deal. The contracts can be very long, with complex issues involved, and you should always hire an attorney to represent you.

ARTIST AND REPERTOIRE

A term you will hear a great deal is *A&R*. This stands for *Artist & Repertoire* and is a fancy term for talent scout for the record label. This person is the one who finds bands and gets them signed to the label. There are people who work in this department for the label, and it will be hard for you to get these people to listen to your material on your own. This is where a manager or attorney who is shopping your CD is a big asset.

The labels also have independent A&R reps who work the local scenes for them. Any time you are approached by someone claiming to be an A&R rep, always check them out. There are plenty of people hanging around your local music scene who will lie about this. When you are approached, always get a business card from them. If it's not a label you have heard of, you will need to ask around. The business card should have not just the rep's direct number, but also the main number for the record label on it. Call that main number and be sure that the label has actually heard of this person. Also, ask yourself if they sound knowledgeable about the business and the label. Another important clue can be the e-mail address. Is it an address that matches the company name or is it some generic, major email site address like AOL, Yahoo, or Hotmail? If it is the latter, you need to check further to be sure the rep really is affiliated with a record label.

Do not waste your time and money wining and dining someone who claims to be a rep without first checking it out, even if you don't do anything that night but call the phone numbers from the card to see how the phones are answered. Even some real independent scouts are way down on the totem pole and may just be looking for a free drink, so don't invest a lot of time and money the first night you meet them on the scene. If you have a manager, tell the rep you will give his or her information to your manager. Also, it should go without saying that you never agree to any kind of deal with a rep. Record labels do not sign bands to great record contracts on the spot.

If you do get an opportunity to get your material before a real A&R rep, make sure your CD is radio ready and you have a professional press pack. This will be the only chance you have to make a good impression with the people at the label who have not seen your shows.

RECOUPMENT

One of the major issues you will have to deal with in any record contract is *recoupment*. Simply put, this clause says that whatever money the record label pays out for your album, your tour support or anything else related to you and your band has to be repaid to the label out of your royalty payments. The monies expended by the label are treated as *advances*—a prepayment of your royalties. The contract will require you to repay these monies first, before any of the royalty money is actually paid to you.

There are many kinds of costs that are covered by this clause. The most obvious one involves the actual cost of recording. If, as a part of your deal, the label is going to be paying for the recording, mixing, and mastering of your album, you will be billed for this money and will pay it back to the label from your part of the sales proceeds of the record.

If you are a hot artist that the label really wants to sign to a deal, the label might agree to pay you a bonus just for agreeing to sign the contract. This signing bonus is an advance that will be repaid from the royalty money.

If the label provides you with any money to help fund a tour to promote your album (*tour support*), this amount is an advance. Video production costs paid by the label are also treated as advances.

In some instances, promotional expenses will be treated as an advance and will be fully recoupable. In other contracts, however, there may be only partial recoupment. If there is a difference in the way these things are treated in your contract, you must be sure the contract adequately defines which expenses are promotions and which are not.

If you already have a recording that the label is going to use (the master), and it has to be bought by the label from a producer or from you, the payment for the master is also an advance.

 Musical Note

Classical music is slightly different in that the labels generally do not require recoupment of recording costs.

For recordings made by union musicians, there are mandatory payments that the label must make to the *Music Performance Trust Fund* (MPTF). You need to pay careful attention to these provisions in your contract because the law exempts the MPTF payments from being classified as recording costs and this payment is not recoupable. Other union payments, however, are recoupable, so watch the contract language carefully.

CROSS COLLATERALIZATION

Another important contractual clause is the *cross collateralization clause*. Simply put, if you owe the record label any money, they can recoup that money out of any royalty money they owe you; even if the costs are owed on one album and they are being recouped from royalties on another. But the clause's reach can actually extend much further.

Under most contracts, the cross collateralization extends to monies owed under other contracts with other entities affiliated with the label. For instance, if you have a contract with the label's publishing company, your share of the publishing monies can be used to recoup costs under the recording contract. This clause can also cover multiple recording contracts with the same company, so that monies owed to the label under a recording contract that has expired can be recouped from a subsequent recording contract.

From the musician's point of view, it would be preferable to negotiate the removal of this clause from the contract completely. However, as a practical matter, you will not be able to achieve this goal. About the most you can hope for is get some limits on it and try not to have too many affiliated contracts, especially with smaller labels when the producer, label, and publishing company are all under the same umbrella.

TERM OF THE AGREEMENT

Every recording contract should contain a provision governing the length of time during which the parties will be bound by the agreement. Because of the way the laws in California are written, you will not see many record contracts that specify a length of time longer than seven years. California law says a contract for personal services is not enforceable after that period of time. However, in a record deal, the contracts muddle the time issue by tying the term to delivery of albums and not just the passage of time on the calendar. Your *year* may be six months after the delivery of your album, regardless of what the calendar says. This is an area of the contract negotiation in which you will definitely need the assistance of a lawyer.

There are many ways you can end up with contract language that has the effect of binding you to the label for longer than seven years. The contract may also contain *option years,* so that the record company can turn a three-year deal into a six-year deal without renegotiating the contract.

RECORDING COMMITMENT

Delivery of an album means that you have gotten the label everything they need to release the album. All of the masters (the recordings), the licenses, the artwork you are providing under the contract, the credits and liner note information, and session tapes have to be to the label in an acceptable form before your album is considered *delivered* under the contract. What you have to deliver is part of your commitment.

Another part of your commitment is the number of albums you must deliver to satisfy your contract. Although this seems to be fairly straightforward, there are some pitfalls to be avoided. Your record contract will contain a clause that states that you will have to deliver some number of masters to the label—the record company will have the right to determine whether or not the masters are acceptable. If the company says that they are not acceptable (either for commercial or technical reasons, depending on the exact language of your contract), then you will have to re-record. If your contract says the label can reject your master for commercial reasons, then the decision-makers at the label have a great deal of discretion as to whether your recordings are sufficient or not.

You also need to watch for contract language about additional albums. This clause can allow the record label to require you to deliver another set of masters of new material so that a second album can be released. Because of the potential problems caused by these clauses, you should try to negotiate a maximum number of masters to be delivered as well as a minimum.

Another issue to keep in mind in this area has to do with the use of live albums. As a general rule, your recording commitment cannot be satisfied by submitting live albums to the label. The contract will require you to submit only masters that are studio recordings.

ROYALTIES

At some point in the process, you are going to want to be paid for your recording efforts. The terms and conditions for those payments are found in the royalty section of the contract. On the surface, the *royalty* is a very simple concept. For every one of your albums the record label sells, they will pay you a percentage. Of course, not much in the music industry is that simple and easy.

Your contract may specify that you are paid a percentage based on the wholesale price, or it may say the retail price. If the percentage is based on wholesale, there will also have to be contract language that sets out how the wholesale price is defined, because not every album will have the exact same wholesale price. For retail based percentages, the issue is whether the rate is based on a suggested retail price, an average of the actual retail prices paid, or based on some formula devised by the label and included in the contract. Generally, your royalty rate on a wholesale-based contract should be about two times larger than the royalty rate based on retail price.

The specific royalty rate you will receive is a matter of negotiation between you and the record company. Rates range anywhere from about 10% to 25%. The newer and less established you are, the lower the rate. You will have to get to the major star level to command a 25% royalty rate. Classical music does not sell as well as other genres, so the royalty percentage is generally lower.

The next issue then becomes what percentage of total sales is used. It might seem obvious to you that you should be receiving your percentage of every album sold by the label, and many contracts will set up your royalty structure this way. However, some contracts contain provisions that say your royalty will be based on a percentage of total sales— usually somewhere between 85% and 90%. If you are presented with one of these contracts, you and your attorney can attempt to change this number during the contract negotiation process.

Your royalty rate may also vary based on the type of recording that is being sold. In most record deals, the basic royalty rate is applied to sales of cassette tapes (and vinyl albums in the old days). Up to this point, this book has been using the terms CDs (for compact discs) and albums interchangeably. In the royalty section of your contract, however, there may be a distinction between your percentage for *albums* (the cassette tapes) and for CDs and other media that may become known in the future. While some contracts pay the same royalty rate for CDs as for albums, other contracts provide for a reduced artist's percentage for CD sales. There will also likely be a clause in the contract that provides for a reduced royalty rate for any technologies that are not known at the time the deal is negotiated but become known during the term of the agreement.

As technology advances, an area of discussion in the royalty area may center around digital downloads. This method of delivery of product dramatically reduces the record label's cost for duplication and shipping, not to mention the elimination of the need for a container for the physical CD.

Because of this, it may become more feasible for artists to negotiate a better royalty structure for downloads, especially as the cost of the technology needed to deliver the CDs electronically decreases.

Your contract will also most likely have separate provisions that deal with the royalties for foreign sales. The actual rate here will vary, depending on the country of sale and the distribution agreements your label has in place in those countries.

Reserve Against Returns

Once you have gotten all the fine points of the royalty calculation resolved, then your contract negotiation proceeds to a section called a *reserve against returns*. Your label will have some sort of return policy in place that lets retail outlets return some portion of the products shipped to the label. As a result of this aspect of the business, your contract will contain a provision allowing the label to hold in reserve some percentage of the royalty monies they owe you so that they can avoid overpayments of your royalties.

If you are presented with a contract that allows the label to hold a *reasonable amount* in reserve, you should attempt to negotiate a fixed percentage for this reserve. If you are a newer artist, especially if you are dealing with a big label, you will have more difficulty getting an agreement on this point, and if you do, the percentage the label holds back will be higher than that of an established artist. If the label will not give you a fixed percentage in the contract, you can request that the reserve against returns number be tied to the Soundscan numbers.

Soundscan is a company that obtains sales information from retail outlets and reports on the sales to labels. (*Billboard* uses this data to compile its charts.) It is the most accurate reflection of the actual number of albums and CDs sold. Since the label should have some idea based on the Soundscan numbers of how many units each retailer has actually sold, there is no reason for their reserve to include units that have already been sold at retail.

Container Charge

The container charge clause is another friend to the record label. This clause permits your record company to withhold money from your royalties to cover the cost of the container in which the tape or CD is encased. This rate is around 20% to 25%, with the higher rate applying to compact discs and the lower to cassette tapes. One area for negotiation on this clause is in regard to electronic delivery of the material. If the CD is being delivered to the end user by digital download, the record company has no container charge that would be applicable to this unit. You can request the record label to exclude all copies of your record that are delivered electronically from the container charge.

You will need to remember the distinction between a record that is *delivered* electronically and one that is *sold* electronically. If the record is sold online but delivered as a physical product in the traditional jewel case, the container charge will still apply.

CONTROLLED COMPOSITION CLAUSE

The controlled composition clause affects those recording artists who are also the writer of one or more of the songs on the album. When this situation arises, the label will ask the artist to accept less than the statutory mechanical rate for the license to record the song. For instance, if the statutory mechanical rate is 8.5¢, the record company might ask you to accept 75% of that amount, or 6.375¢. If you are the sole writer of two songs on the album, you would receive 12.75¢ for each album sold (6.375¢ per song times two songs). As your career becomes more profitable for the label, they may be willing to negotiate a better deal for you in this area.

Other Reductions

Your record company will need to be able to pass out free copies of your album for promotional purposes and your contract will give them the right to do so. You will not be paid any royalties on these albums. You do need to be sure, though, that any free copies that are returned are not counted as a return, as this will reduce your royalty a second time for the same unit. Your contract will also reduce your royalty payments for albums sold at a significant discount for pro-motional purposes (called *premium records*), for records sold at a very low price after the album has lost its sales steam (a *budget record*), and for records sold at a price that is about halfway between the suggested retail price and the budget price (a *midline record*). The only tool you have to control these items in any way is to try to negotiate a limit on how and when these activities can take place.

Coupling and Compilations

Coupling and compilations involve joining your performance with the performances of other artists. If you have two songs on a compilation CD that contains a total of twelve songs, then your royalty will be ⅙ of the total royalty.

RELEASE OF THE RECORD

In most cases, the record company will initially present you with a contract that does not contain a provision requiring them to ever release the recordings you deliver to them. Since you do not want to be bound forever to a record company that owns your masters but will not release them, you should negotiate for a clause that provides for a buy-back of the masters. If you cannot get an agreement on this point, you need to at least have a clause that lets you terminate the contract with the label if they refuse to release the record. If you are successful in getting one of these clauses added to your contract and find yourself in the position of needing to use it, read it very carefully. Most clauses like this will have notice provisions, and there will be deadlines involved. If you do not send the correct notices at the correct time, you could lose your right to get out of the contract.

MISCELLANEOUS CONTRACT PROVISIONS

In addition to the contract provisions that have been discussed up to this point, there are several more that deserve some mentioning. A few of them are highlighted here.

Suspensions

Many recording contracts will have a clause that permits the company to suspend the artist. If a suspension clause is exercised, this means that the artist is suspended from recording for the company. The contract will allow the clause to be used when the artist is in breach of contract. An artist can be in breach of contract if he or she fails to deliver the recordings in a timely manner or if he or she is unable or unwilling to perform.

When you are suspended, the record company will not permit you to record for them, and your contract prohibits you from recording for anyone else, so you are stuck in limbo until the suspension is lifted. You cannot just sit out the suspension and wait for the contract term to end either, because your contract will probably state that any time period that you are suspended gets added to the contract term. If you have a four year deal, you get suspended during year two, and your suspension lasts for one year, you now have to be under contract to the label for five years instead of four (to you make up the suspension time to the company).

The contract will also generally contain a *force majeure* clause, which temporarily suspends the contract if one of the parties is unable to perform its contractual obligations because of something outside his or her control, such as an act of God. In addition, the contract will also contain a clause that sets out the circumstances under which the label can terminate the agreement.

Name Changes

Your record company is not going to want to spend a great deal of money promoting your band and its material, and developing the music industry version of brand identification, only to have your band decide it wants a different name. Therefore, there may be a clause in your contract that keeps you from changing the name of the band without the label's consent.

Audits

The contract should always contain provisions related to the providing of accountings by the label to the artist. Every company will have some sort of basic accounting period, and at the end of each period, they will provide a royalty statement to the artist. Most often, that period is every six months, so you will receive your royalty statement and payments within a specified time period after June 30 and December 31 of each year.

Not every company follows this same schedule, though, so you will need to know what your contract says about this requirement. You should also make certain that your contract has a clause in it that allows you to audit the record label if you believe that you are not getting all the money to which you are entitled. Although you are unlikely to ever use this clause, it is still important to have this remedy available to you, because you never know what problems may arise in the future. You will have to pay for the audit, which is very time-consuming, and therefore, very expensive.

Permission

As previously discussed, if you use part of a recording made by someone else on your record (called *sampling*), you have to have a license to use it. Your contract with the record label will make you responsible for obtaining all the necessary permissions and authorizations. If you do this incorrectly and the label gets sued, your contract will make you responsible for repaying the label for any money they must expend as a result of the lawsuit. This is called the *indemnification provision*.

Grant of Rights

Every record contract will contain clauses about the *grant of rights*. You should read this section of the contact carefully and go over it thoroughly with your lawyer. These provisions are very important because they govern the ultimate ownership of your material, including the ownership of the copyrights. Be sure you understand exactly what it is you are giving up to the record company before you sign the agreement.

Re-Recording

Most record contracts also contain what is called a *re-recording provision*. This clause says that you cannot record any of the material that you have recorded under your contract with the label for anyone else for a specified time period after the expiration of your contract.

Affiliate Labels

One clause that you, as the artist, will want to try to have included in the contract is a clause committing the record company to specify which one of their labels it will use to release your material. That helps to prevent you from being shunted off to a minor label within the major label family, which can be important because the minor label may not give you as much promotional support.

MERCHANDISING RIGHTS

When you are negotiating your deal with the record company, they may ask you to assign merchandising rights to them. Since the band may be able to make more money from the sale of merchandise than from the recording royalties, you may not want to assign those rights. This is an important area of negotiation, and you should not give up these rights without careful consideration.

VIDEOS

Another contract item that may be part of your negotiation has to do with video productions. Your contract will address whether the label will be paying for a music video to promote your album or not. If there will be a label-funded video, the amount allocated for production will be determined by the label.

Until you are a more established artist, the company may not be willing to do a video. The contract will leave that decision to the discretion of the company. As your status grows, you may be able to get a video commitment from the label added into the contract. For the most part, the creative decisions about your video will be made by the label, although you will get a little bit more input if you become more of a star.

SIDEMAN CLAUSES

If you ever want to play on any other artist's record, you should be sure your contract includes a *sideman clause* that lets you do so. Otherwise, the exclusive nature of the recording contract may keep you from being able to participate.

DEVELOPMENT DEALS

There is another type of contract labels sometimes offered to artists when they are not willing to offer the full deal. This interim arrangement is called a *development deal*, or *demo deal*. In this scenario, the label gives the artist a small budget to do a basic recording. (They generally will not pay for mastering and the budget is limited, so the mixing, by definition, is also more limited.) There will be fewer songs on the demo as well. The purpose of this development deal is for the label to get an idea of the artist's sound on a professional recording. If the label likes the demo, then a more extensive contract will be offered.

If you and the company cannot reach agreement on a deal, or if they do not offer a deal based on the demo, then you can shop the demo to other record labels. If you get an offer from one of them, most development contracts will require you to come back to the company that funded the demo. The funding company will have the right to make you sign a deal with them as long as they offer you the same terms as the deal you got from the new record company. If the funding label refuses to match your offer, then you can sign your contract with the new label. However, your contract with the company that funded the demo will require you to reimburse them for the money they paid for the demo out of the money you get from the record deal based on that demo.

Privately Financed Demos

If your demo is financed by a private third party individual or company instead of a record company, be sure that you have a written agreement with this person or company. It is important to address what rights the financier is getting. If you do not, you may find that he or she will try to take ownership and control of your record, or claim to be owed a percentage of any record deal you get. Be sure that the contract requires him or her to provide you with an account and documentation of the amount of financing he or she provided so that you know how much he or she is owed. Also, be sure the contract is clear on how the repayment will occur.

PRODUCERS

A producer is the person hired, either by the record company or the band, to do the actual recording, mixing, and mastering of the record. If the same person is going to produce the entire album, then the term of his or her contract will be the same as the term of the recording contract. The other alternative is for a term of a specific number of songs, or just one song, depending on the particulars of the deal.

Most producer's contracts will include provisions for a production fee, which will either be a flat fee for the project or may vary based on the amount of songs produced. Depending on how the contract is worded, the production fee may or may not be treated as an advance. The difference is that an advance is recoupable from the producer's royalties, while a flat fee is not. This fee is separate and in addition to the producer's royalties.

The contract with the producer will also address recording costs. As a general rule, the recording costs are not recoupable from the producer's royalty. This, of course, is different than the provisions applicable to the artists who must repay the recording costs from their royalties.

The average royalty for a producer is 3% to 4% of the retail price. Most independent producers have contracts that include what is called a *record one clause*, meaning they get paid royalties beginning with the very first record sold. The producers generally have to wait until the recording costs have been recouped from the artist, but then the royalties are paid retroactive to the first record sold.

The producer's basic job is to make your band sound as great as possible. There are several areas in which the producer can help—by helping you structure your songs to fit your audience or to have mass appeal, by helping play up the *hooks* in your song (the hook is the actual lyric or melody, which is generally repeated in the song and that catches the listener's ear and makes your song memorable), by giving your recording radio quality, and by ensuring that your songs meet radio standards. Generally, for radio, your songs should be about three and a half minutes long and the first verse should begin no later than about twenty seconds into the song.

If you are picking your own producer, try to work with someone who has worked with a national artist or a local artist who has been signed to a label deal. Listen to other recordings that producer has done. If they sound bad, yours probably will too. If some of the recordings are good and others are bad, you may want to keep looking for a producer whose work quality is more consistent. Also, be sure you are working with an actual producer. Many people who run small local studios are not producers but are simply sound engineers. There is more to producing that just knowing how to set up the microphones and record. A good producer knows the tricks of the trade to help you get the best sound on your recording and knows when to apply those techniques and when not to.

LOAN OUTS

If you are using a musician on a recording that is signed to a label other than yours, that other label will have to give its permission. When this happens, your CD label and liner notes will have to reflect that fact. It will say that *musician x is appearing courtesy of label y*. If the musician is playing live with you, you will want to identify that person as *label y recording artist x* when you introduce the band.

chapter thirteen:
Doing Business with an Independent Label

In the previous chapter, issues relating to recording contracts were covered. For the most part, it focused on how those issues are handled when you are dealing with one of the major labels or one of the smaller labels owned by the majors. The issues in recording are similar when dealing with an independent (or *indie*) label, but the way the issues are handled is different in many ways.

When you sign with a major label, you may be paid an advance, which will then have to be recouped from your royalties. While some indie labels will pay an advance, many will not. This is often because these small labels do not have the budget to pay artists any kind of substantial advance, at least until the label begins to receive funds from the sale of the album.

Another fact of life when doing business with a smaller label is that the label will not just agree to pay all of your recording costs. Because of budget limitations, most small indies will do what is called an *all-in deal*. This means that they will allocate a specific dollar amount to you as a recording budget. It is then up to you to get the album made within the budgeted amount. The label will not just turn this money over to you, either. They will monitor, approve, and pay each individual expense as it arises.

Distribution is another area of significant difference between indies and majors. The majors do all of their own distribution. The independents that are owned and operated by the majors, while they may not have their own in-house distribution, have access to the distribution network at their major label. Most indies, however, do not do their own distribution. In order for your record to get into the retail marketplace, the indie label will have to enter into some sort of contract with a distributor. Any time you are considering signing a recording agreement with an indie label, you must always ask about the distribution arrangements. You need to know who the distributors will be and what retail channels are available to your record under the contract. You also need to know how much the distribution is going to cost you. Without this information, you cannot accurately evaluate whether the offer you are considering is viable or not.

You may also run into small labels that will not have any significant money in the budget to give you for your recording. However, do not let this fact by itself keep you from doing business with that label, especially if that label has sufficient connections to help your material get distributed and noticed. Also, remember that you can often make more money from modest sales through a small label than you can with a bigger sales volume through a major. This is because your royalty percentage and related terms may be more favorable with the small label.

Royalties are often handled in different ways with an independent label. While some of the larger indies operate are more like the majors, other indies will treat the relationship with the artist as more of a partnership. In practical terms, this means that the label and the artist will equally split the profits from the sale of that artist's album. If you are negotiating a contract with an indie that takes that approach, you want to pay attention to the language in the contract that defines what exactly it is that gets split. If you sign a contract with language stating that the profits are split, then you may have a problem getting any money out of your record. You

 Musical Note

If the indie is aggressive in its accounting practices, the balance sheet (at the end of the day) may show that there have been no profits from your album sales to split. This may happen even if the album has sold hundreds of thousands of copies.

want the contract to specify what items can be deducted from the gross sales receipts (the money from sales of your record before anything is taken out) to get to the profit number.

You also want to watch out for contracts with indie labels that provide for cross collateralization, especially when the indie label, the producer of the record, and the publishing company are owned by the same person or people. While indie labels generally have the reputation of being more artist-friendly than the majors, you still have to recognize that there are indie labels out there that are just as good as the major labels at separating you from your royalty money.

ACTING AS YOUR OWN LABEL

One way to truly be dealing with an independent label is for the artist to essentially act as his or her own label. If you plan to take this step, you will need to be prepared to operate this venture as a separate business. For liability purposes, if you are serious about releasing your own work and getting it into distribution (and maybe even signing other artists to your label), you should incorporate your label. For more information about incorporation and setting up a business, see Chapter 1.

If you are just issuing your own CD because you are a new band and need something to use for promotional purposes, you do not need to take on the extra responsibility and expense of creating a new business. You just need to be sure that your CD label, album artwork, and liners comply with the copyright laws and do not infringe on anyone else's copyright.

chapter fourteen:
The Record and CD Duplication Business

If you are signed to a label deal, you will not have to worry about finding a duplication company and getting copies of your record made. The record company handles all of this for you. However, if you are issuing your CD yourself, you have to know how this part of the process works.

MAKING THE MASTER

The first step is to have your recording mixed and mastered. When you record, the various instrumental and vocal parts are each recorded on a separate track. The tracks are then combined to create the sound that is your song. *Mixing* refers to the process of adjusting the volume levels of each track in each part of the song so that the final recording, when played, sounds like you want it to sound. *Mastering* (sometimes called postproduction) is the final process in which the mix is put into final form—called the *master*. If you want your recording to sound professional, then you need to spend the extra money to have it mixed and mastered.

You will also need to decide on exactly what configuration you want to use for the CD—full length, EP, or a single. An

EP is a CD that contains more than one song but fewer than the number of songs found on a full-length version. Most demos are EPs because they contain only four or five songs.

DUPLICATION

Once you decide what you want to produce, you have to select a company to perform the duplication services. Some duplication companies will also master the recording for you, so you should check with several companies to see what services are available and what the costs are for those services. Other information you will need from the duplication company in order to make an informed decision involves minimum order requirements, delivery time, and turnaround time on reorders. Once you have the answers to all of these questions, you can decide which company provides you the best service at the best price.

You will then submit either your mixed or mastered recording, along with the album art, CD label, and liner information you want to use, to the duplication company. It will be less expensive for you if the artwork is camera-ready. *Camera-ready* means the art is ready to be reproduced exactly as it is with no additional work needed by the printer.

When you get ready to have your CD pressed (duplicated), you should get some sample copies from the duplication company so that you know how the final version is going to sound. If there is a problem with the sound or the mastering done by the company, it is better to find out this information before your order of 1,000 has been shipped to you and you have to pay for it.

BAR CODES

The next decision you need to make is whether to bar code your CD or not. If you are not going to try for a recording deal and you are just going to give your CDs away at shows as an advertising method, then you do not need to take the time or incur the expense. However, if you want a label deal at some point in the future or you want to put your CD into distribution, then you should get the bar code. When your manager or attorney is shopping your recording to a label, it is helpful to have the statistics on how many records you have sold. Having a bar code system helps you keep track of your inventory so you can provide accurate records on what you have sold directly. In order to have distribution into retail outlets, you have to have the bar code. The information from the bar code helps the retailer keep track of inventory. It is also what is used by Soundscan to calculate sales amounts.

In order to use a bar code, you have to first obtain a manufacturer's number from the Uniform Code Council. This number will go on every bar code of every one of your products. Then, you will assign each product its own identification number to put on the bar code after the manufacturer number. The product ID is your own internal inventory number—only the manufacturer number is on file with the Uniform Code Council.

There is a fee for the manufacturer number. The amount of the fee depends on what your expected sales revenue is and the number of products you will be coding.

 Musical Note

The Uniform Code Council can be found at:

www.uc-council.org

If you have questions, you can contact them at:

info@uc-council.org
937-435-3870

The Council website recommends that you complete the online application and submit it. They will let you know what the fee will be. Once they quote the fee to you, you still have the option of canceling the transaction before any payment information is submitted. It takes about three to five days to receive your number. At that point, you can use commercially available software to print your own bar codes. There are also firms that can be found online who will print this for you. For your CDs, the duplication firm will be responsible for putting the codes onto the packaging.

chapter fifteen:
Selling Your CDs and Merchandise

Now that you have a CD that looks and sounds good, you have to sell it. Of course, you can sell copies at your shows and to your friends and family members. You may even be able to convince a local store or two to carry the CD. However, if you want to get your CD into any of the big chain stores and have it available nationally, you will need some sort of distribution method.

DEALING WITH DISTRIBUTORS

If your CD was produced under a contract with a major label or one of the smaller labels owned by a major, distribution will be part of your contract with the label and you will not have to worry about finding distribution. Even if you are signed to a small indie label, the company will likely be the one to select the distributor and deal with the legal and business aspects. If you are doing your own label, it will be up to you to secure a distribution deal. Whether you are finding your own deal or have the benefit of a deal already in place through your record label, you need to understand the issues related to distribution.

There are generally two kinds of distributors—regional distributors and national distributors. Some of the national distributors are owned by the major labels and some are independent distributors who work with indie labels.

Regardless of the scope of the distributor's operation, the job of the distribution company is to get the finished product (your CD) into the retail system, to process the returns (CDs that do not sell can be returned by the stores), to collect your money from the retailers, and to pay you for the sales. There are some distributors who will get involved in the process earlier and do what is called a *P&D deal*. P&D stands for pressing and distribution. This means that the distribution company will actually front the expenses for pressing the CDs and recoup their money from the sales revenues. Distributors are paid on a percentage of sales, generally in the neighborhood of 20% to 30%.

If you are just issuing your own CD (as opposed to starting your own actual label with other artists signed to it), you will not have much success getting a distribution deal with one of the bigger distributors. They are looking for labels with a decent size roster of artists. You will have to focus your efforts on the small, local distributors.

While you should not be afraid to deal with smaller regional distributors, you will want to know what stores are part of their distribution network. If they have a small network, you will have limited product availability. However, they may still be able to get you into any local independent record stores or other smaller stores that sell CDs.

You can also get online distribution by using a company like *CD Baby*. They will sell your CD for you online, either by shipping a physical CD that you provide them or by digital download. To sell your physical CDs, you pay a one-time fee of $35 per title to set up the account, and CD Baby keeps $4 per CD sold. You set the retail sales price of the CD. While they do not require bar coding to sell your CD through their website, they will report to Soundscan if you have it coded. For digital downloads, they keep 9% of the download price. They can be found at **www.cdbaby.com**.

PROMOTING YOUR MATERIAL

If you are signed to a record deal, the label will help you to promote your CD and will have a promotions budget to help with that process. If you have done your own CD or are starting your own label, then you either have to do the promoting yourself or hire a promotions company to do some of it for you.

The first step will be to schedule a show and have a CD release. If you are a local band, try to book your release show into the venue that has been the most favorable for you in terms of draw and audience response. If you are a touring band, you can schedule a tour around the release of your new CD.

In advance of the CD release show, be sure to advertise the show heavily. Use the same methods you use to promote any other show—posters in the venue and in other locations around town that are music fan friendly and will let you advertise there. Be sure you pass out as many flyers as you can in and around the music scene, starting at least two weeks before the show. You should have a mailing list, so send notice of the show to everyone on the list. If you have a local paper that focuses on the music scene, you can purchase ad space and advertise the CD and the release show. If you can afford it, you can also buy ad time on the radio.

While you are in this process, do not forget college papers and radio stations in your area.

If you are going to tour—even to just a few cities—to promote your record, you will need to follow the same steps in each city. Of course, you will not be able to personally be in each city two weeks before the show, so you will need a street team. The street team, a group of individuals hired by the band to promote shows, can pass out the flyers and put up the posters. You do not have to pay large sums of money to the people on the *street team*, but you will need to offer them something for the work they do on your behalf, perhaps a small amount of money, free merchandise, or free show tickets.

The fact that you will need a street team makes it important for the band to network within the industry—especially within the local music scene. Since your street team will be made up primarily of fans, you need to get to know as many of them as possible. That way, they can refer their friends in other cities to you and help you build a network of street teams around the area in which you will be playing.

You can also try to get radio play for your song. This will be easier if you have a local station in your genre that is friendly to local, unsigned bands, or one that hosts a local music show. This is another area in which networking can help, because you still have to be able to get the right people at the station to hear your music.

If you have a management company, your manager will also be able to help you in this area. Your manager will have his or her own network of contacts and promotions ideas. Even with a management company on your team, you may want to hire a professional promotions company to help you get radio play. Getting onto a station's playlist, especially a commercial station, is not an easy task. You might also consider searching online for Web radio stations and approaching them about playing your music. Another online resource is **www.myspace.com** where you can create a profile and advertise your new CD.

You will want to have CDs with you to sell at each show. You will need some sort of inventory control system so you can keep track of how many CDs you have, how many you sold, and how much money you have been paid.

If you have done your own CD and do not have to account to any third party financing sources, you can also consider giving some of your CDs away to help increase your fan base. You may lose some money on those particular CDs, but gain in the long run by creating a larger base of potential customers.

 Musical Note

It is also important to work with your booking agent so your performance dates are booked around the time of your CD release. Your performance dates are significant components of the promotion's plan that you, your manager, and label have developed.

By this point in the process, your band should already have a press kit. The press kit should contain a brief history of the band and short biography of the members, along with a photo and a CD, now that you have one.

The individual band members can also take CDs and go to stores themselves to ask if the store will carry the CD. Take several copies with you and ask to speak to the manager. Of course, you will need to target stores into which your music will fit and in which fans of your type of music are likely to shop.

One of the most important places for promoting your CD is the band's website. Be sure to promote the fact that it is being released well in advance to help build anticipation among the fans who visit the site. When it is released, advertise that fact and include links and instructions for purchasing copies. Ideally, your website will be set up so that people can order the CD online from your site and have it shipped directly to them. If you are technologically sophisticated enough or hire a company to help you with this process, you can design software that enables the CD to be purchased and downloaded online.

BOOTLEGS

Regardless of whether your CD is on a major label or you record it yourself, bootleg copies of it will be a problem. Encrypting your online versions will make it harder to illegally download, but staying ahead of the technology is a big job. As a practical matter, it takes an organization as big as the *Recording Industry Association of America* (an industry group for labels) to go to court and litigate against illegal downloaders.

SELLING YOUR MERCHANDISE

Along with CDs, your band should develop and maintain a line of merchandise. When you are just starting out, you do not need a merchandise line the size of a retail outlet. Just some basic items will be sufficient. T-shirts, baseball caps, stickers, key chains, and koozies make a good starting lineup. Since merchandise will be sold primarily at shows at this stage in your career, you need to make arrangements for someone trustworthy to staff your merchandise booth at each show.

Your merchandise line should also be available for purchase from your website. If you are not set up to sell online from your site, there are companies that will produce your merchandise and ship it directly to the customer through a link on your site. As your career advances, you will have enough demand for your products that you will have the option of hiring a merchandise company to handle this part of your business for you. Merchandise companies work a little bit like record companies. You license to them the right to use your likenesses (your pictures) and your band's name, and they create the merchandise.

They may pay you an advance, which has to be recouped, and you get paid on a royalty basis, which is a percentage of the items sold. The merchandisers will handle both the merchandise that is sold at your shows and get your items into retail distribution. Remember that once you begin performing at larger venues, they will also be taking a percentage of the money made from the product sales that occur at the venue.

One area of potential concern is that of a *conflict of interest*. If you are dealing with more than one merchandising company (for example, if you have a regional retail deal with one company and a touring merchandise deal with another), be sure that each contract allows for sales to occur under the other. If, for example, your regional retail deal prohibits any other sales within a fifty-mile radius and you play a show in the area, your at-show sales violate your contract with the regional distributor. The reverse may also be true—your regional retail sales may violate your contract with the tour merchandiser. Be sure to have your attorney negotiate each deal in such a way that your ability to enter into the other deal is preserved.

Record Keeping

There is an important part of this process that many bands do not focus on enough—the record keeping. You are going to have to file a tax return, and you need to account for the money made from the sales. The IRS is not going to just take your word for how much money came in and how much you paid for the products you sold. *You need to keep records.* When you purchase things to sell, keep the receipt. When you are selling at shows, create an inventory log that lists how many of each item was given to your sales staff that night, how many were returned after the show, and how much money you took in. Have the sales person sign this sheet of paper. It does not have to be fancy, but it is important.

You may also be able to get some of your merchandise into a retail setting by approaching local record stores and other local music friendly retailers. You will need the same sort of documentation for them, because if they take your merchandise, they will most likely be taking it on *consignment.* They will expect you to have records of how much you left with them, how much you picked up that did not sell, and how much they owe. When you drop the merchandise off at the store, have the employee who accepts it sign the inventory sheet so that you can prove how much of your merchandise the store had in the event of a dispute.

chapter sixteen:
Doing Business on the Internet

In today's world, no discussion of the music business would be complete without the Internet. The Web is an important tool when it comes to marketing your band, and you really need to have a presence there.

THE BAND WEBSITE

The first step to getting a website is securing the domain name. When you selected the name of your band, you should have checked to see if that domain name or one close to it was available. You will get the right to use the name by reserving it on one of the websites that provides this service. Fees vary depending on which company you choose and what other services (like Web hosting and email) you choose.

Once your name is reserved, you will need to get the site itself designed. You want the site to have a clean, professional appearance,

 Musical Note

The rights to your domain name are very important. Any time you are negotiating a contract (such as with a record label), be sure that there is not anything in the contract that gives away the rights to this name.

and from a technical standpoint, not be so complex that the site loads slowly and people lose interest. Unless you have a band member or friend who has experience as a Web designer, you should consider getting some professional help with the design of your site.

In terms of content, there are some basic items that every site needs to have. You want a photograph—one that fits with the genre of music you play, but not one that is so *artistic* that you cannot see the faces of the musicians. There should also be a brief history of the band and a short biography of each member.

You should always have contact information on the site. If you have a management company and booking agent, their names, addresses, and phone numbers should be listed. If you are fulfilling these responsibilities yourself, then put your name and phone number on the site.

You should also consider including an electronic press kit on the site so that prospective employers (either venues, record labels, or concert promoters) can download it. The electronic press kit will probably contain much of the same information found throughout your site, but it will be grouped together so potential employers can easily download one item. Your site should have a calendar section listing your upcoming show dates. Many sites also include a forum so fans and band members can post messages.

Most sites for bands also include either all or part of some of the band's songs. Somewhere between one and three songs is sufficient for this purpose. It is important in designing this portion of the site to be sure you know how to encrypt the site so that the audio cannot be downloaded for free from your site.

Website Basics

At a minimum, your band's website should include the following:

❏ a calendar with your upcoming show dates;

❏ media-audio clips and video if you have it;

❏ a forum;

❏ a bio of the band;

❏ contact information for booking and management, if you have a manager;

❏ a news section to pass along information to your fans;

❏ a section that allows fans to sign up for your email list (so that you can send out emails to your fans promoting your shows and CDs);

❏ links to any sponsors or record labels with which you do business; and,

❏ for a more sophisticated site, you can include an e-store to sell CDs and merchandise, a sign up section for fans who want to be on your street team, or a chat feature.

There are, of course, license issues that go along with the audio clips. If the audio is streaming (just played but not downloaded), then that is a performance of the music and a performance license fee is payable to the performance rights society (ASCAP, BMI, SESAC), unless a direct license has been obtained from the copyright owner. If the audio is downloadable, then a mechanical royalty payment is owed. If the site includes video that accompanies the audio, then a synchronization license is required.

Music played over the Internet also involves *Sound Exchange*. Sound Exchange is an organization that is somewhat similar to ASCAP, BMI, and SESAC, but it deals strictly with royalties payable as a result of electronic delivery of music online. Sound Exchange pays royalties for songs that are digitally downloaded. In order to receive royalties from them, you must be registered with them. (For more information about Sound Exchange, see Chapter 8 or go to their website, **www.soundexchange.com**.)

OTHER ONLINE OPPORTUNITIES

Another online opportunity for your band is to create a Web log, or *blog*. You can post information about your band on the blog and have a dialogue with fans.

There are lots of other sites that you can access to give your band an Internet presence. You should search the web for some of the many sites that will sell your CDs for you. Do not forget about Web magazines that review music and Web radio stations. Many of the Web stations are very friendly to independent bands not signed to any record deals. For more information on music related websites, go to **www.indiebible.com**.

chapter seventeen:
Taxes

Unfortunately, no book about the business aspects of any-thing would be complete without a discussion of taxes—and a book about the music industry is no different. There are several different tax-related issues, some personal income tax issues and some business tax issues. While a whole book could be devoted to this topic, only some highlights are presented here.

BAND TAXES

There are several ways in which tax consequences arise from the operation of the band. Every time the band plays a show for money, a taxable event has occurred. If you are performing as a solo artist, then the money you make from shows is personal income to you and is reported on your tax return on Schedule C of *Form 1040*.

You will have to complete Schedule C—the schedule for self-employed business owners—because your musical career is considered a business when you get paid for playing. Because it is a business, you should keep all of your receipts for related expenses so that you can deduct those expenses from the money you make playing. This will help reduce the amount of money you owe in taxes.

Because you are self-employed, you also have to pay the full amount of Social Security and Medicare taxes yourself. When you work for someone else, your employer pays half of these taxes and you pay the other half. When you are self-employed, you pay 15.3% of 93.25% of the amount of profit from your business operations for this tax. If you live in a state with a state income tax, you will have to pay those taxes as well on the profits from your musical performances.

If your band operates as a partnership, the partnership has to file an informational tax return. The partnership itself does not pay federal income taxes. The profit made by the partnership flows through to the individual partners, and they pay taxes on their portion of the taxes. The amount of income that must be claimed by each partner is determined by the tax reporting form given to that partner. The partnership determines this amount based on the total number of partners or through your written partnership agreement. For example, if the partnership made a $100,000 profit for the year and there are four partners, each partner will pay personal income tax on $25,000. You will need to check the laws of your state to determine what the state tax rules are that apply to your situation.

If the band is incorporated, the corporation files a federal income tax return and pays federal income taxes based on the profit earned by the corporation at the corporate tax rate. Any money that was paid out to the band members will be reported either as regular income—meaning the band members get a *W-2* form—or as a stock dividend.

The corporation has to pay its part of the Social Security and Medicare taxes for each employee (including the band members), and withhold for federal income tax liability on any money paid to the band members that would be defined as a *salary*. This is true for partnerships with employees as well as corporations. The business has to deposit any withholding payments with the government on a quarterly basis and file a report.

You will need the assistance of a tax professional to help your business (the band) determine how payments are handled and what the consequences of each method are, both for the members personally and for the band as an entity. The band members pay taxes based on the amounts in the *W-2* just like employees of any other company. There will also be state tax issues as well, since most states have some sort of corporate income tax or franchise tax fees that must be paid. As always, the individual band members need to know what the laws of their home state are in regard to personal income taxes.

Because you must file these reports, you will need each employee's tax identification number, which is generally their Social Security number. For that reason, you should have every new employee complete a Form *W-9*, which requests their taxpayer identification number, and keep this form in your business files. You must also complete Form *I-9* for each employee. This is the document used to verify the citizenship or legal resident status of your employees. This must be done to comply with the immigration laws.

Most states require all businesses with employees to pay some sort of unemployment tax as well. This tax provides the money to fund unemployment compensation payments. Your tax rate will usually be based on your history as an employer. As a new business, you will pay based on what kind of business you are and the fact that you are new. When you have been in business for a while, your tax rate will change based on your record. If you have many former employees filing unemployment claims, your rate will go up. If you have no claims on your record, your rate will gradually decrease to a minimum rate.

Money you make from your CDs is also taxable income. If the band is a partnership or corporation, and the money comes from a deal with a record label, the sales royalty monies will be payable to the band as a business. You also need to have each employee complete a *W-4* form, which is the form used to designate the number of dependent exemptions the employee claims. This number affects the amount of taxes withheld, and you must get this form before you pay them any money. It is also the form that you can use to report each *new hire* to the state, as discussed in Chapter 1. The record label will provide the necessary tax forms to the band, and you will complete your own forms based on what you get from the label. The income will be treated like the income from performances and taxed accordingly.

If the band has produced the recording itself, then be sure to keep all the documentation and receipts related to the costs of creating and marketing the recording. These costs can be deducted from the income made from the sale of the CD, which reduces your tax liability.

There are some complicated issues related to taxation of recording income and treatment of expenses. There are rules in place regarding depreciation in regard to recordings and how expenses may be deducted. Therefore, if you have income or expenses in this area, you should get professional help in preparing your tax return.

If the band sells merchandise, the income from the merchandise sales is taxable income as well. If you have done your own merchandise, be sure to keep accurate records in this area. Your supply of T-shirts, stickers, and other merchandise is inventory, and you have to be able to account for how much you have made from your sales and how much it cost you to create the goods you sold. If you are dealing with a merchandiser, that company will keep these types of records and will provide you with a tax reporting form that you will use to prepare the personal and business tax returns.

DEDUCTIONS

As soon as you begin playing for money, you need to keep track not just of your income, but also of all of your expenses. Keep receipts for everything you buy related to your music career, so that you can deduct the expenses from your income and reduce the amount of taxes you owe. You can deduct things like:

- equipment purchases directly related to the band;
- hotel room costs at out-of-town shows;
- gas costs to get to shows;
- meals for out-of-town shows;
- the money you paid to buy the merchandise you sell;
- fees you pay to the professionals on your team (your manager, business manager, booking agent, and attorney);
- crew and band salaries (remember, though, that even when the band members' salaries are a deduction for the corporation, it is still taxable income to the individual member);
- insurance premiums you pay for band-related items such as workers' compensation; and,
- rent paid on the band's practice room.

If you are doing your own booking of shows, you may also be able to deduct phone costs to the extent that your phone is used for business purposes.

SONGWRITING INCOME

The characterization of income from songs you have written depends on how the income was derived. If there is no publishing deal, and you are just getting performance royalty payments from ASCAP or BMI, that is generally just regular income to you. It will probably be personal income to you and the other songwriters and will not go through the band's records, unless the band entity is the copyright owner.

If you have a publishing deal that involved the transfer of ownership of your copyright, then some additional rules apply. The transfer of your copyright is the sale of an asset for tax purposes, and any profit from the sale of the asset is taxable. Depending on whether you are the one who created the copyrighted material or purchased or inherited the right from someone else, your income may be treated differently. Non-creators are engaging in the purchase and sale of a capital asset and may be able to use the capital gains tax rates to reduce the tax liability. This is not available to copyright owners who created the work. This is another area in which the advice of a tax professional is extremely valuable.

Tax laws change all of the time. You should seek the advice of a tax advisor for the most current rules and regulations affecting your band.

TAX AND ESTATE PLANNING

If your career takes off and you make significant money from your music, you will need tax and other financial advice to help you develop strategies to reduce your tax payments. You should set up retirement plans when you reach this stage of your career. There are two main reasons for this. First, the money you put into retirement accounts in your peak earning years helps reduce your tax liability in those years. Second, you are creating financial security for yourself and your family, since the number of big earning years for most artists is limited.

As your financial status improves, you need to be aware of estate planning. If you have a net worth of more than one million dollars, your family will likely have to pay estate taxes when they inherit your property (depending on the year in which you die). Good advance planning can eliminate these tax payments entirely. Consult an attorney in this area because you will need a will and other legal documents.

Conclusion

Now that you have finished the book, you are equipped to handle the basics of the business of music. With the right music and the right stage show combined with the right team around you, you can take your shot at stardom. Even if you don't make it that far, you can still enjoy a successful career as a professional musician.

Glossary

A

advance. A pre-payment of royalties.

arrangement. Transcription into print music.

American Society of Composers, Authors, and Publishers (ASCAP). Performance rights society.

B

BMI. Performance rights society.

booking. Process of scheduling a live performance.

booking agent. Person who arranges for musicians to play at venues.

business manager. Person who handles financial affairs.

C

compulsory license. The right of others to use the work once a song has been exploited.

copyright. The statutory device for ownership of creative works such as songs.

copyright infringement. Act that violates the ownership interest in a creative work.

cover. Song written by one person and performed by another.

cross collateralization. The right, given in a contract, to be repaid money advanced on one project from the monies received from other projects.

D

door. Total amount of money paid by people to see a particular show.

draw. The number of people who pay to see a show.

E

EP. A CD that has more than one song, but fewer than a full-length CD.

exploit. To use a creative work for commercial purposes.

G

genre. A particular type of music; rock or country, for example.

I

indie. Record label other than a major label, shorthand for independent label.

L

license. Right to use a creative work of another person.

M

manager. Person who advises a musical act in matters related to their career. Also called a personal manager.

master. Two meanings. 1. The post-production work on a recording. 2. The final version of the recording itself.

master use license. The right to use a particular recording made by someone else.

mechanical license. The right to record a song written by another person.

mechanical royalty. The payment to the songwriter for each sale of a recording made pursuant to a mechanical license.

mixing. The process of adjusting the sound levels of the various tracks of a recording to create a desired sound for a song.

P

performance agreement. The contract that contains the terms for a live appearance by a musical act.

performance rights society. Organization that administers royalty payments earned by songwriters when other people play their song.

phonorecord. The term used in the *Copyright Act* for a recording, such as a CD.

public domain. A creative work with no copyright protection.

publishing. The process of licensing songs for commercial use.

R

recoup. Process of repayment of money advanced, such as for recording or merchandise creation.

rider. Addendum to a performance agreement containing special requirements of the musical act as a condition for performing.

royalty. Fee paid for sales of recordings or use of songs.

S

sampling. Digitally copying a sound from another recording.

SESAC. A performance rights society.

service mark. Identifying name or design to identify and distinguish one service provider from another. Like a trademark except applies to services and not goods.

Sound Exchange. Organization that administers royalty payments for digitally downloaded material.

Soundscan. Company that collects data from sales of recordings. Used to determine the *Billboard* charts.

statutory rate. The amount set by law as the royalty rate for a compulsory mechanical license.

street team. Group who provides promotional services to a musical act, such as passing out flyers advertising shows.

synchronization license. The right to use a song accompanied by video images. Also called a synch license.

T

talent agent. *See booking agent.*

tour support. Money advanced by record label to pay for series of shows played by an act to promote a recording.

appendix:
Sample Forms

In any endeavor, there are going to be numerous forms you have to complete. Some are necessary as you start a new business, some are used when you book a gig, and some are required by governmental entities to register your rights. This appendix provides several samples of some of the forms and documents you are likely to come across. These forms contain blanks where you would provide your own specific information, but do not use these documents for anything more than a reference.

While some are copies of forms the IRS or Copyright Office require of you, others are only examples that, depending on the state you are in, may or may not be exactly applicable. However, all of the forms and accompanying material should assist you in knowing what to look for and include in any agreement you execute.

Table of Forms

ARTICLES OF INCORPORATION
OF
_____, Inc

ARTICLE ONE
The name of the corporation is _____, Inc.

ARTICLE TWO
The period of its duration is perpetual.

ARTICLE THREE
The purpose for which the corporation is organized is the transaction of any and all lawful business for which corporations may be incorporated under the Texas Business Corporation Act.

ARTICLE FOUR
The aggregate number of shares which the corporation shall have the authority to issue is _____ of par value of one dollar each.

ARTICLE FIVE
The corporation will not commence business until it has received for the issuance of shares consideration of the value of One Thousand Dollars ($1,000.00).

ARTICLE SIX
The street address of its initial registered office is _____, and the name of its initial registered agent at such address is _____.

ARTICLE SEVEN

The number of directors constituting the initial board of directors is _____ (__), the names and addresses of the persons who are to serve as directors until the first annual meeting of the shareholders or until their successors are elected and qualified are:

_____

_____

_____

_____

_____

_____

_____

_____

ARTICLE EIGHT

The name and address of the incorporator is:

_____

_____

_____

Signed on: _____

BYLAWS
OF
_____, INC.

ARTICLE I - OFFICES

1. REGISTERED OFFICE AND AGENT

The registered office of the corporation shall be maintained at _____.
The name of the registered agent of the corporation at such address is _____.
The registered office or the registered agent, or both, may be changed by resolution of the Board of Directors, upon filing the statement required by law.

2. PRINCIPAL OFFICE

The principal office of the corporation shall be at _____ _____, provided that the Board of Directors shall have power to change the location of the principal office in its discretion.

3. OTHER OFFICES

The corporation may also have other offices at such places, within or without the State of Texas, where the corporation is qualified to do business as the Board of Directors may from time to time designate, or as the business of the corporation may require.

ARTICLE II - SHAREHOLDERS

1. PLACE OF MEETING

All meetings of shareholders, both regular and special, shall be held either at the registered office of the corporation in

Texas or at such other places, either within or without the state, as shall be designated in the notice of the meeting.

2. ANNUAL MEETING

The annual meeting of shareholders for the election of directors and for the transaction of all other business which may come before the meeting shall be held prior to the end of each fiscal year at the time and place set by the directors.

If the election of directors shall not be held at the annual meeting of shareholders, the Board of Directors shall cause the election to be held as soon thereafter as convenient. The election may be at a special meeting of the shareholders called for the purpose of holding such election.

The annual meeting of shareholders may be held for any other purpose in addition to the election of directors which may be specified in a notice of such meeting. The meeting may be called by resolution of the Board of Directors or by a writing filed with the Secretary signed either by a majority of the directors or by shareholders owning a majority in amount of the entire capital stock of the corporation issued and outstanding and entitled to vote at any such meeting.

3. NOTICE OF SHAREHOLDERS' MEETING

Notice of all meetings of shareholders shall be given in writing to shareholders entitled to vote by the President or Secretary or by the officer or person calling the meeting, or, in case of his neglect or refusal, or if there is no person charged with the duty of giving notice, by any Director or shareholder. The notice shall be given to each shareholder, either personally or by prepaid mail, addressed to the shareholder at his address appearing on the transfer books of the corporation.

Notice of any meeting of shareholders shall be sent to each shareholder entitled thereto not less than ten (10) nor more than sixty (60) days before the meeting, except in the case of a meeting for the purpose of approving a merger or conversion agreement, in which case the notice must be given not less than twenty (20) days prior to the date of the meeting.

Notice of any meeting of shareholders shall specify the place, date, and hour of the meeting. The notice shall also specify the purpose of the meeting if it is a special meeting, or if its purpose, or one of its purposes, will be to consider a proposed amendment of the Articles of Incorporation, to consider a proposed reduction of stated capital without amendment, to consider a proposed merger or conversion, to consider a voluntary dissolution or the revocation of a voluntary dissolution by act of the corporation, or to consider a proposed disposition of all, or substantially all, of the assets of the corporation outside of the ordinary course of business.

When a shareholders' meeting is adjourned for thirty (30) days or more, notice of the adjourned meeting shall be given as in the case of an original meeting. When a meeting is adjourned for less than thirty (30) days, it is not necessary to give any notice of the time and place of the adjourned meeting or of the business to be transacted thereat other than by announcement at the meeting at which the adjournment is taken.

Subject to the notice provisions required by these Bylaws and by the Business Corporation Act, shareholders may participate in and hold a meeting by means of conference telephone or similar communications equipment by which all persons participating can hear each other. Participation in such a meeting shall constitute presence in person at such meeting, except participation for the express purpose of objecting to the transaction of any business on the ground that the meeting is not lawfully called or convened.

Any notice required by law or by these Bylaws may be waived by execution of a written waiver of notice executed by the person entitled to the notice. The waiver may be signed before or after the time stated in the notice.

4. SPECIAL SHAREHOLDERS' MEETINGS

Special meetings of the shareholders, for any purpose whatsoever, may be called at any time by any of the following: (a) the President; (b) the Board of Directors; (c) one or more shareholders holding not less than one tenth of all the shares entitled to vote at the meetings; and (d) the Executive Committee.

Any person or persons entitled hereunder to call a special meeting of shareholders may do so only by written request sent by registered mail or delivered in person to the President or Secretary. The officer receiving the written request shall within ten days from the date of its receipt cause notice of the meeting to be given in the manner provided by these Bylaws to all shareholders entitled to vote at the meeting. If the officer does not give notice of the meeting within ten days after the date of receipt of the written request, the person or persons calling the meeting may fix the time of meeting and give the notice in the manner provided in these Bylaws. Nothing contained in this section shall be construed as limiting, fixing, or affecting the time or date when a meeting of shareholders called by action of the Board of Directors may be held.

5. VOTING OF SHARES

Each outstanding share, regardless of class, shall be entitled to one vote on each matter submitted to a vote at a meeting of shareholders, except to the extent that the voting rights of the shares of any class or classes are limited or denied by the Articles of Incorporation or by law.

Shares of its own stock owned by a corporation or by another domestic or foreign corporation or other entity, if the majority of the voting stock or voting interest of the other corporation or other entity is owned or controlled by this corporation, shall not be voted, directly or indirectly, at any meeting, and shall not be counted in determining the total number of outstanding shares at any given time.

A shareholder may vote either in person or by proxy executed in writing by the shareholder or by his duly authorized attorney in-fact. No proxy shall be valid after eleven (11) months from the date of its execution unless otherwise provided in the proxy. Each proxy shall be revocable unless expressly provided therein to be irrevocable, and in no event shall it remain irrevocable for a period of more than eleven (11) months.

At each election for directors every shareholder entitled to vote at such election shall have the right to vote, in person or by proxy, the number of shares owned by him for as many persons as there are directors to be elected and for whose election he has a right to vote, or unless prohibited by the Articles of Incorporation, to cumulate his votes by giving one candidate as many votes as the number of such directors multiplied by the number of his shares shall equal, or by distributing such votes on the same principal among any number of such candidates. Any shareholder who intends to cumulate his votes as herein authorized shall give written notice of such intention to the Secretary of the corporation on or before the day preceding the election at which such shareholder intends to cumulate his votes. If any shareholder gives written notice as provided above, all shareholders may cumulate their vote.

6. QUORUM OF SHAREHOLDERS

Unless otherwise provided in the Articles of Incorporation, for any matter to be presented, the holders of a majority of the shares entitled to vote at the meeting, represented in person or by proxy, shall constitute a quorum at a meeting of shareholders, but in no event shall a quorum consist of the holders of less then one-third (⅓) of the shares entitled to vote at the meeting and thus represented at such meeting. The vote of the holders of a majority of the shares entitled to vote on, that voted for or against or expressly abstained with respect to the matter at the meeting and thus represented at a meeting at which a quorum is present shall be the act of the shareholders' meeting, unless the vote of a greater number is required by law, the Articles of Incorporation or the Bylaws.

7. CLOSING TRANSFER BOOKS AND FIXING RECORD DATE

For the purpose of determining shareholders entitled to notice of or to vote at any meeting of shareholders or any adjournment thereof, or entitled to receive payment of any dividend, or in order to make a determination of shareholders for any other proper purpose, the Board of Directors may provide that the share transfer books shall be closed for a stated period not exceeding sixty (60) days. If the stock transfer books shall be closed for the purpose of determining shareholders entitled to notice of or to vote at a meeting of shareholders, such books shall be closed for at least ten (10) days immediately preceding such meeting. In lieu of closing the stock transfer books, the Bylaws or in the absence of an applicable bylaw the Board of Directors, may fix in advance a date as the record date for any such determination of shareholders, not later than sixty (60) days and, in case of a meeting of shareholders, not earlier than ten (10) days prior to the date on which the particular action, requiring such determination of shareholders is to be taken. If the share transfer books are not closed and no record date is fixed for the determination of shareholders entitled to notice of or to vote at a meeting of shareholders, or shareholders entitled to receive payment of a dividend, the date on which notice of the meeting is mailed or the date on which the resolution of the Board of Directors declaring such dividend is adopted, as the case may be, shall be the record date for such determination of shareholders. When a determination of shareholders entitled to vote at any meeting of shareholders has been made as provided in this section, such determination shall apply to any adjournment thereof, except where the determination has been made through the closing of share transfer books and the stated period of closing has expired.

8. VOTING LISTS

The officer or agent having charge of the share transfer books for the shares of the corporation shall make, at least ten (10) days before each meeting of shareholders, a complete list of the shareholders entitled to vote at such meeting or any adjournment thereof, arranged in alphabetical order, with the address of and the number of shares held by each, which list, for a period of ten (10) days prior to such meeting, shall be kept on file at the principal office of the corporation and shall be subject to inspection by any shareholder at any time during usual business hours. Such list shall also be produced and kept open at the time and place of the meeting and shall be subject to the inspection by any shareholder during the whole time of the meeting. The original share transfer books shall be prima-facie evidence as to who are the shareholders entitled to examine such list or transfer books or to vote at any meeting of shareholders. However failure to prepare and make the list available in the manner provided above shall not effect the validity of any action taken at the meeting.

ARTICLE III - DIRECTORS

1. BOARD OF DIRECTORS

The business and affairs of the corporation and all corporate powers shall be exercised by or under authority of the Board of Directors. Directors need not be residents of the State of Texas or shareholders in the corporation. Directors when used in relation to any power or duty requiring collective action means "Board of Directors."

2. NUMBER AND ELECTION OF DIRECTORS

The number of directors shall be two (2) provided that the number may be increased or decreased from time to time by an amendment to these Bylaws, but no decrease shall have the effect of shortening the term of any incumbent director. At each annual election the shareholders shall elect directors to hold office until the next succeeding annual meeting.

The entire Board of Directors or any individual Director may be removed from office by a vote of shareholders holding a majority of the outstanding shares entitled to vote at an election of Directors. However, if less than the entire Board is to be removed, no one of the Directors may be removed if the votes cast against his removal would be sufficient to elect him if then cumulatively voted at an election of the entire Board of Directors. If any or all Directors are so removed, new Directors may be elected at the same meeting. Whenever a class or series of shares is entitled to elect one or more Directors under authority granted by the Articles, the provisions of this paragraph apply to the vote of that class or series and not to the vote of the outstanding shares as a whole.

3. VACANCIES

Any vacancy occurring in the Board of Directors may be filled by the affirmative vote of the remaining directors, though less than a quorum of the board. A director elected to fill a vacancy shall be elected for the unexpired term of his predecessor in office. Any directorship to be filed by reason of an increase in the number of directors shall be filled by election at the annual meeting or at a special meeting of shareholders called for that purpose. A reduction of the authorized number of Directors shall not remove any Director prior to the expiration of that Directors' term of office.

4. ANNUAL MEETING OF DIRECTORS

Within thirty days after each annual meeting of shareholders, the Board of Directors elected at such meeting shall hold an annual meeting at which they shall elect officers and transact such other business as shall come before the meeting.

5. REGULAR MEETING OF DIRECTORS

A regular meeting of the Board of Directors may be held at such time as shall be determined from time to time by resolution of the Board of Directors.

6. SPECIAL MEETINGS OF DIRECTORS

The Secretary shall call a special meeting of the Board of Directors whenever requested to do so by the President or by two directors. Such special meeting shall be held at the time specified in the notice of meeting.

7. PLACE OF DIRECTORS' MEETINGS

All meetings of the Board of Directors (annual, regular or special) shall be held either at the principal office of the corporation or at such other place, either within or without the State of Texas, as shall be specified in the notice of meeting.

8. NOTICE OF DIRECTORS' MEETINGS

All meetings of the Board of Directors (annual, regular or special) shall be held upon five (5) days' written notice stating the date, place, and hour of meeting delivered to each director either personally or by mail or at the direction of the President or the Secretary or the officer or person calling the meeting.

In any case where all of the directors execute a waiver of notice of the time and place of meeting, no notice thereof shall be required, and any such meeting (whether annual, regular or special) shall be held at the time and at the place (either within or without the State of Texas) specified in the waiver of notice. Attendance of a director at any meeting shall constitute a waiver of notice of such meeting, except where the directors attend a meeting for the express purpose of objecting to the transaction of any business on the grounds that the meeting is not lawfully called or convened.

Neither the business to be transacted at, nor the purpose of, any annual, regular or special meeting of the Board of Directors need be specified in the notice or waiver of notice of such meeting.

9. QUORUM OF DIRECTORS

A majority of the Board of Directors shall constitute a quorum for the transaction of business. The act of the majority of the directors present at a meeting at which a quorum is present shall be the act of the Board of Directors.

10. COMPENSATION

Directors, as such, shall not receive any stated salary for their services, but by resolution of the Board of Directors a fixed sum and expenses of attendance, if any, may be allowed for attendance at each annual, regular or special meeting of the board, provided, that nothing herein contained shall be construed to preclude any director from serving the corporation in any other capacity and receiving compensation therefor.

11. MEETINGS BY TELEPHONE CONFERENCE OR OTHER REMOTE COMMUNICATIONS TECHNOLOGY

Subject to the provisions for notice required by these Bylaws and the Business Corporation Act for notice of meetings, Directors may participate in and hold a meeting by means of conference telephone or similar communications equipment by which all Persons participating in the meeting can hear each other. Or, another suitable electronic communications system may be used including videoconferencing technology or the Internet, but only if, each Director entitled to participate in the meeting consents to the meeting being held by means of that system and the system provides access to the meeting in a manner or using a method by which each Director participating in the meeting can communicate concurrently with each other participant. Participation in such meeting shall constitute attendance and presence in person at such meeting, except where a Person participates in the meeting for the express purpose of objecting to the transaction of any business on the ground that the meeting is not lawfully called or convened.

12. EXECUTIVE COMMITTEE

The Board of Directors may at any time appoint from among its members an executive committee and one or more other committees, each of which so appointed shall have such power and authority to conduct the business and affairs of the corporation as is vested by law, the Articles of Incorporation, and these Bylaws in the Board of Directors as a whole, except that it may not take any action that is specifically prohibited to the Board of Directors by statute or that is specifically required by statute to be taken by the entire Board of Directors. Members of the executive committee shall receive such compensation as the Board of Directors may from time to time provide. Each Director shall be deemed to have assented to any action of the executive committee unless he shall, within seven (7) days after receiving actual or constructive notice of such action, deliver his written dissent thereto to the Secretary of the corporation. Members of the executive committee shall serve at the pleasure of the Board of Directors.

The Board of Directors, by an affirmative vote of a majority of the members constituting the Board of Directors, may appoint other committees which shall have and may exercise such powers as shall be conferred or authorized by resolution of the Board. A majority of any such committee may determine its action and fix the time and place of its meetings unless the Board of Directors shall otherwise provide. The Board of Directors, by such affirmative vote, shall have power at any time to change the powers and members of any such committees, to fill vacancies, and to dispose of any such committee.

ARTICLE IV - OFFICERS

1. OFFICERS ELECTION

The officers of the corporation shall consist of a President, one or more Vice-Presidents, a Secretary, and a Treasurer. All such officers shall be elected at the annual meeting of the Board of Directors provided for in Article III, Section 4. If any office is not filled at such annual meeting, it may be filled at any subsequent regular or special meeting of the board. The Board of Directors at such annual meeting, or at any subsequent regular or special meeting may also elect or appoint such other officers and assistant officers and agents as may be deemed necessary. One person may hold two or more offices.

All officers and assistant officers shall be elected to serve until the next annual meeting of directors (following the next annual meeting of shareholders) or until their successors are elected; provided, that any officer or assistant officer elected or appointed by the Board of Directors may be removed with or without cause at any regular or special meeting of the board whenever in the judgment of the Board of Directors the best interests of the corporation will be served thereby, but such removal shall be without prejudice to the contract rights, if any, of the person so removed. Any agent appointed shall serve for such term, not longer than the next annual meeting of the Board of Directors, as shall be specified, subject to like right of removal by the Board of Directors.

2. VACANCIES

If any office becomes vacant for any reason, the vacancy may be filled by the Board of Directors.

3. POWERS OF OFFICERS

Each officer shall have, subject to these Bylaws, in addition to the duties and powers specifically set forth herein, such powers and duties as are commonly incident to that office and such duties and powers as the Board of Directors shall from time to time designate. All officers shall perform their duties subject to the directions and under the supervision of the Board of Directors. The President may secure the fidelity of any and all officers by bond or otherwise.

4. PRESIDENT

The President shall be the chief executive officer of the corporation and shall preside at all meetings of all directors and shareholders. Such officer shall see that all orders and resolutions of the board are carried out, subject however, to the right of the directors to delegate specific powers, except such as may be by statute exclusively conferred on the President, to any other officers of the corporation.

The President or any Vice-President shall execute bonds, mortgages and other instruments requiring a seal, in the name of the corporation. When authorized by the board, the President or any Vice-President may affix the seal to any instrument requiring the same; and the seal when so affixed shall be attested by the signature of either the Secretary or an Assistant Secretary. The President or any Vice-President shall sign certificates of stock.

The President shall be ex-officio a member of all standing committees.

The President shall submit a report of the operations of the corporation for the year to the directors at their meeting next preceding the annual meeting of the shareholders and to the shareholders at their annual meeting.

5. VICE-PRESIDENTS

The Vice-President, or Vice-Presidents in order of their rank as fixed by the Board of Directors, shall, in the absence or disability of the President, perform the duties and exercise the powers of the president, and they shall perform such other duties as the Board of Directors shall prescribe.

6. THE SECRETARY AND ASSISTANT SECRETARIES

The Secretary shall attend all meetings of the board and all meetings of the shareholders and shall record all votes and the minutes of all proceedings and shall perform like duties for the standing committees when required. The Secretary shall give or cause to be given notice of all meetings of the shareholders and all meetings of the Board of Directors and shall perform such other duties as may be prescribed by the Board of Directors. The Secretary shall keep in safe custody the seal of the corporation, and when authorized by the board, affix the same to any instrument requiring it, and when so affixed, it shall be attested by the Secretary's signature or by the signature of an Assistant Secretary.

The Assistant Secretary shall in order of their rank as fixed by the Board of Directors, in the absence or disability of the Secretary, perform the duties and exercise the powers of the Secretary, and they shall perform such other duties as the Board of Directors shall prescribe.

In the absence of the Secretary or an Assistant Secretary, the minutes of all meetings of the board and shareholders shall be recorded by such person as shall be designated by the President or by the Board of Directors.

7. THE TREASURER AND ASSISTANT TREASURERS

The Treasurer shall have the custody of the corporate funds and securities and shall keep full and accurate accounts of receipts and disbursements in books belonging to the corporation and shall deposit all moneys and other valuable effects in the name and to the credit of the corporation in such depositories as may be designated by the Board of Directors.

The Treasurer shall disburse the funds of the corporation as may be ordered by the Board of Directors, taking proper vouchers for such disbursements. The Treasurer shall keep and maintain the corporation's books of account and shall render to the President and directors an account of all of his transactions as Treasurer and of the financial condition of the corporation and exhibit the books, records, and accounts to the President or directors at any time. The Treasurer shall disburse funds for capital expenditures as authorized by the Board of Directors and in accordance with the orders of the President, and present to the President for his attention any requests for disbursing funds if in the judgment of the Treasurer any such request is not properly authorized. The Treasurer shall perform such other duties as may be directed by the Board of Directors or by the President.

If required by the Board of Directors, the Treasurer shall give the corporation a bond in such sum and with such surety or sureties as shall be satisfactory to the board for the faithful performance of the duties of the office and for the restoration to the corporation, in case of death, resignation, retirement, or removal from office, of all books, papers, vouchers, money, and other property of whatever kind in the incumbent's possession or under the incumbent's control belonging to the corporation.

The Assistant Treasurers in the order of their seniority shall, in the absence or disability of the Treasurer, perform the duties and exercise the powers of the Treasurer, and they shall perform such other duties as the Board of Directors shall prescribe.

ARTICLE V -
SHARES: STOCK CERTIFICATES, ISSUANCE, TRANSFER, ETC.

1. CERTIFICATES OF STOCK

The certificates for shares of stock of the corporation shall be numbered and shall be entered in the corporation as they are issued. They shall exhibit the holder's name and number of shares and shall be signed by the President or a Vice-President and the Secretary and shall be sealed with the seal of the corporation or a facsimile thereof. If the corporation has a transfer agent or a registrar, other than the corporation itself of an employee of the corporation, the signatures of any such officer may be facsimile. In case any officer or officers who shall have signed or whose facsimile signature or signatures shall have been used on any such certificate or certificates shall cease to be such officer or officers of the corporation, whether because of death, resignation, or otherwise, before said certificate or certificates shall have been issued, such certificate may nevertheless be issued by the corporation with the same effect as though the person or persons who signed such certificates or whose facsimile signature or signatures shall have been used thereon had been such officer or officers at the date of its issuance. Certificates shall be in such form as shall in conformity to law be prescribed from time to time by the Board of Directors.

The Board of Directors may appoint from time to time transfer agents and registrars, who shall perform their duties under the supervision of the Secretary.

Neither shares nor certificates representing shares may be issued by the corporation until the full account of the consideration has been paid. When the consideration has been paid to the corporation, the shares shall be deemed to have been issued and the certificate representing the shares shall be issued to the shareholder.

2. TRANSFERS OF SHARES

Upon surrender to the corporation or the transfer agent of the corporation of a certificate for shares duly endorsed or accompanied by proper evidence of succession, assignment or authority to transfer, it shall be the duty of the corporation to issue a new certificate to the person entitled thereto, cancel the old certificate, and record the transaction upon its books.

3. REGISTERED SHAREHOLDERS

The corporation shall be entitled to treat the holder of record of any share or shares of stock as the holder in fact thereof and, accordingly shall not be bound to recognize any equitable or other claim to or interest in such share on the part of any other person, whether or not it shall have express or other notice thereof, except as otherwise provided by law.

4. LOST CERTIFICATE

The Board of Directors may direct a new certificate or certificates to be issued in place of any certificate or certificates theretofore issued by the corporation alleged to have been lost or destroyed, upon the making of an affidavit of that fact by the person claiming the certificate to be lost. When authorizing such issue of a new certificate or certificates, the Board of Directors in its discretion and as a condition precedent to the issuance thereof, may require the owner of such lost or destroyed certificate or certificates or his legal representative to advertise the same in such manner as it shall require or to give the corporation a bond with surety and inform satisfactory to the corporation (which bond shall also name the corporation's transfer agents and registrars, if any, as obligees) in such sum as it may direct as indemnity against any claim that may be made against the corporation or other obligees with respect to the certificate alleged to have been lost or destroyed, or to advertise and also give such bond.

ARTICLE VI - DIVIDEND

1. DECLARATION

The Board of Directors may declare at any annual, regular, or special meeting of the board and the corporation may pay, dividends on the outstanding shares in cash, property or in the shares of the corporation to the extent permitted by, and subject to the provisions of, the laws of the State of Texas.

2. RESERVES

Before payment of any dividend there may be set aside out of any funds of the corporation available for dividends such sum or sums as the directors from time to time in their absolute discretion think proper as a reserve fund to meet contingencies or for equalizing dividends or for repairing or maintaining any property of the corporation or for such other purpose as the directors shall think conducive to the interest of the corporation, and the directors may abolish any such reserve in the manner in which it was created.

ARTICLE VII - MISCELLANEOUS

1. INFORMAL ACTION

Any action required to be taken, or which may be taken at a meeting of the shareholders, directors, or members of the executive committee, may be taken without a meeting if a consent in writing setting forth the action so taken shall be signed by all of the shareholders, directors, or members of the executive committee, as the case may be, entitled to vote with respect to the subject matter thereof, and such consent shall have the same force and effect as a unanimous vote of the shareholders, directors, or members of the executive committee, as the case may be, at a meeting of said body.

2. SEAL

The corporate seal shall be circular in form and shall contain the name of the corporation, the year of its incorporation and words "TEXAS," and "CORPORATE SEAL" or an image of the Lone Star. The seal may be used by causing it or a facsimile to be impressed or affixed or in any other manner reproduced. The corporate seal may be altered by order of the Board of Directors at any time.

3. CHECKS, DRAFTS, ETC.

All checks, drafts, or other instruments for payment of money or notes of the corporation shall be signed by such officer or officers or such other person or persons as shall be determined from time to time by Resolution of the Board of Directors.

4. FISCAL YEAR

The fiscal year of the corporation shall be as determined by the Board of Directors.

5. DIRECTORS' ANNUAL REPORT TO SHAREHOLDERS

The Board of Directors shall present at each annual meeting of shareholders a full and clear statement of the business and condition of the corporation.

ARTICLE VIII - AMENDMENT OF BYLAWS

Bylaws may be altered, amended, or repealed, and new bylaws may be adopted, by the Directors, subject to repeal or change by action of the shareholders.

Adopted by the Board of Directors on _____.

_____
Secretary

ATTEST:

_____
Director

_____
Director

BOOKING AGREEMENT

This agreement is made and entered into as of the _____ day of _____, 20_____, by and between _____ (hereinafter referred to as "Agent") and _____ (hereinafter referred to as "Artist"). In consideration of the mutual covenants and agreements contained in this agreement, the parties hereby agree as follows:

1. Engagement and Term

Artist engages Agent to render services to Artist in the entertainment field to obtain employment for Artist as a musical act for a period of _____, beginning on the effective date of this agreement as set out above.

Artist agrees to pay Agent compensation for such services as set out below.

2. Scope of Agreement and Limitation of Authority

Agent shall be an independent contractor and, as such, Artist shall not be required to withhold taxes from monies paid to Agent. Agent is authorized to make representations only as set forth in Agent's company regulations manual or as Artist directs by written or oral communications.

Agent has no authority to act for or on behalf of Artist except as provided for in this Agreement; no other authority, power, or use is granted or implied.

Agent may not incur any debt, obligation, expense, or liability of any kind against Artist other than the debts, obligations, expenses, and liabilities customarily incurred against Artist in the ordinary course of booking engagements and securing employment for Artist without Artist's written consent.

Artist and Agent agree to comply with all local, state, Federal, and foreign laws and regulations applicable to the transactions between Artist and Agent or third parties involved in this agreement and the performance agreements between Artist and any contractors retaining Artist's services.

3. Termination of Agreement

If, after the term of this agreement has expired, the parties continue to do business together as if this agreement were still in effect, the practices constitute a renewal of the agreement until one of the parties notifies the other in writing of the termination. The letter of termination must give thirty (30) days notice to the other party.

Termination is upon the expiration of the term set out above or by agreement of the parties, or immediately upon the breach of this agreement by either party. A breach of this agreement includes but is not limited to violation of the policies and rules of the Agent or Artist, the making of a misrepresentation or false statement by Agent or Artist, nonperformance of Artist's duties, cancellation by Artist without cause of any engagements arranged for Artist by Agent, the death of Artist, failure by Agent to secure bona fide offers of employment for Artist for a period of four consecutive months, conditioned on Artist being ready, willing, and able to perform at all times during the four month period, or the occurrence of a conflict of interest between Agent and Artist. In the event of a breach, the nonbreaching party shall be entitled to compensation as set out below. Any termination that results from any condition other than the expiration of the term of the agreement or the completion of the engagement covered by this agreement shall require thirty days written notice to the other party. In the event employment is secured after the expiration of the four month period set out above and prior to the giving of the written notice, neither party shall be entitled to terminate the agreement based on that clause.

4. **Duties**

Agent hereby agrees to use all reasonable diligence and reasonable efforts to secure employment for Artist. Artist agrees to be ready, willing, and able to perform at all times during the term of this agreement and to use its best efforts in any engagement arranged by Agent. Artist shall be relieved of its obligation to be available to perform in the event of an act of God, fire, catastrophe, labor disagreement between third parties making it impossible for Artist to perform, acts of government or its agencies, any order, regulation, ruling, or action of any labor union or association affecting the entertainment industry.

Artist agrees that Agent shall be its sole booking agent and that Artist will not make any performance arrangements or represent its availability to perform or undertake any negotiations for performances on its own behalf. Artist shall promptly notify Agent of any requests for its services or inquiries about its availability received directly to Agent.

5. **Compensation**

As compensation for Agent's services hereunder, Artist shall pay to Agent as and when received by Artist _____ percent (___%) of the compensation paid to Artist for each regular engagement arranged for Artist by Agent. In the event that any engagement is canceled by either party to the performance contract, Agent shall be entitled to receive ten percent (10%) of the contractual amount that was to be paid to Artist under the performance agreement.

The parties agree and it is hereby understood that Agent shall not be liable to Artist for any payments owed to Artist by the venue or contractor or other party to the performance agreement negotiated for Artist by Agent. It is further agreed that Agent shall have no liability to any third parties for acts and/or omissions of Artist or breaches of any performance agreement by Artist, specifically including but not limited to cancellation fees imposed against Artist, and Artist shall fully indemnify and hold Agent harmless from any such liability.

If Agent negotiates employment for Artist during the term of this agreement, Agent shall be entitled to compensation under this agreement even if the engagement actually occurs after the termination of this agreement.

6. **Expenses**

All reasonable expenses (other than Agent's fixed office expense or other general overhead) actually incurred by Agent on Artist's behalf, including but not limited to long distance and toll telephone charges, long distance facsimile charges, messenger fees, travel expenses, and any other disbursement made on Artist's behalf shall be paid by Artist. If Agent, at Agent's election, initially advances the funds for said expenses, Artist shall reimburse Agent for said expenses. Agent shall submit an itemized statement to Artist and Artist shall pay said expenses within fifteen days of the submission of the itemized statement. Upon Artist's request, Agent shall make available to Artist or Artist's designated representative during regular business hours on no more than one occasion per statement the underlying documentation supporting the claimed expenses.

7. **Warranties and Representations**

Artist warrants that it is a partnership authorized to do business in Texas and that it is free to enter into this contract and to grant to Agent the rights contained in this agreement, that the individual or individuals signing this agreement on Artist's behalf have the full authority to sign binding contracts for Artist, and that no obligations exist that would conflict with any of the provisions of this agreement. In the event that Artist incorporates, Artist agrees to adopt all necessary resolutions to ratify this agreement and to thereafter maintain its corporate status in good standing. Agent warrants that it is free to enter into this agreement and that no obligations exist that would conflict with any of the provisions of this agreement. Nothing contained herein shall obligate either party to pay any of the other party's personal or corporate indebtedness and neither party shall be responsible or liable for any unlawful acts, torts, or breaches of contract committed by the other party. In the event that either party does not fully perform or cause to be performed any agreement or obligation undertaken by that party, or commits any unlawful act, tort, or breach of contract, that party agrees to indemnify and hold harmless the other party from any and all claims, demands, actions, judgments, and awards against the party failing to perform or committing the act or omission giving rise to the claim.

8. **Miscellaneous**

In the event any dispute arises under this agreement that results in litigation or arbitration, the prevailing party shall be paid its reasonable attorney's fees and costs by the losing party. This agreement and any attachments or riders incorporated herein shall be governed by the laws of the State of Texas may be modified only in signed writing, and is binding and valid only when signed by both parties. All obligations are to be performed in Dallas County, Texas. Venue shall be exclusively in Dallas County, Texas.

This agreement shall be binding upon and inure to the benefit of the parties and their respective heirs, executors, administrators, legal representatives, successors, and assigns. Neither party shall have the right to assign or transfer their obligations under this agreement without the written consent of the other party. It is understood and agreed that Agent's services under this agreement shall be non-exclusive.

If any party to this agreement is a legal entity (partnership, corporation, or trust), that party represents to the other that this agreement, the transaction contemplated in this agreement, and the execution and delivery of this agreement, have been duly authorized by all necessary partnership, corporate, or trust proceedings.

Time is of the essence in this agreement and all time limits shall be strictly construed and enforced.

The failure or delay in the enforcement of the rights detailed in this agreement by either party shall not constitute a waiver of those rights or be considered a basis for estoppel. The parties may exercise their rights under this agreement despite the delay or failure to enforce those rights.

The paragraph headings used in this agreement are descriptive only and shall have no legal force or effect.

If any provision of this agreement shall, for any reason, be held violative of any applicable law or be otherwise unenforceable, the invalidity of such provision shall not be held to invalidate any other provision in this agreement, which other provisions shall remain in full force and effect unless removal of the invalid provision destroys the legitimate purposes of this agreement, in which event this agreement shall be canceled.

This agreement represents the entire agreement between the parties except as otherwise provided in this agreement, and it may not be changed except by written amendment duly executed by all of the parties.

Artist and Agent acknowledge that they have each had the opportunity to consult legal counsel of their own choosing and at their own expense to advise each of them in connection with the execution of this agreement and that each has either engaged such counsel or freely and voluntarily waived their right to do so. The parties acknowledge and agree that neither Agent nor any of Agent's attorneys has provided any legal services or advice to Artist in connection with this agreement.

SIGNED, ACCEPTED, AND AGREED TO by the undersigned parties, who hereby acknowledge that they have read and understood this agreement and that each hereby executes this legal document voluntarily and of their own free will.

Agent:

_____

By:_____

Dated:_____

Artist:

_____

By:_____

Dated:_____

Dated:_____

_____

Dated:_____

_____

Dated:_____

_____

PERFORMANCE AGREEMENT

This agreement is made and entered into as of [contract date] by and between _____[venue name]_____ (hereinafter referred to as Contractor) and _____[band]_____, (hereinafter referred to as Artist). In consideration of Artist's performance at the venue assigned by Contractor, the parties agree as follows:

1) Artist shall perform an engagement at__[venue name]__ on ____[gig date]____ consisting of _____ sets and lasting for approximately ____[performance length]____. Contractor agrees that Artist shall be permitted to take the stage to begin its performance no later than ___ p.m. If other musical acts are scheduled to perform on the same night, Artist and Contractor agree that Artist shall be the opening/headlining/# ___ act in the performance order.

2) Contractor agrees to pay Artist as follows:
   _____ The sum of $_____ as a guaranteed fee.
   _____ ___% of the gross of the following items:
   ____ ticket sales
   ____ door receipts
   ____ bar receipts
   ____ other receipts as follows: _____
   _____
   _____.
   ____ club scale
   ____ greater of club scale or $_____

If Artist is to be paid a guaranteed fee in addition to a percentage fee, the guaranteed fee shall be a minimum payment and shall be paid to Artist on or before _____. Any and all remaining payments shall be paid to Artist's manager or other person authorized in writing by Artist's manager to receive payment at the close of Artist's performance.

3) Additional terms are as follows:

Load in time is _____.

Set up and sound check time with full access to stage and P.A. equipment shall be _____.

Backstage security provided by Contractor.

Cover charge/ticket price shall be _____.

Age limits at the performance are _____.

Artist shall be entitled to _____ number of free tickets.

Artist shall have the option to sell albums, CDs, books, and/or other merchandising material at the performance and shall retain all proceeds of such sales.

Artist shall have the right to place promotional materials advertising its performance in the venue up to two weeks prior to the date of the performance.

4) Cancellation

If Contractor cancels Artist's performance under this agreement for any reason other than an act of God, fire, catastrophe, labor disagreement between third parties making it impossible for Contractor to perform, acts of government or its agencies, any order, regulation, ruling, or action of any labor union or association affecting the entertainment industry within thirty days of the scheduled date, Contractor shall pay a cancellation fee to Artist of $__[cancel fee]__, due and payable within 5 days of the notice of cancellation. If Artist cancels its performance under this agreement for any reason other than an act of God, fire, catastrophe, illness of the Artist, labor disagreement between third parties making it impossible for Contractor to perform, acts of government or its agencies, any order, regulation, ruling, or action of any labor union or association affecting the entertainment industry within thirty days of the scheduled date, Artist shall pay Contractor a cancellation fee of $__[cancel fee]__, due and payable within five days of the notice of cancellation.

SIGNED AND ACCEPTED:

Contractor: _____[venue name]_____

_____

Artist: _____[band]_____

_____

Form **SS-4**	**Application for Employer Identification Number**	EIN

Form **SS-4**
(Rev. December 2001)
Department of the Treasury
Internal Revenue Service

Application for Employer Identification Number
(For use by employers, corporations, partnerships, trusts, estates, churches, government agencies, Indian tribal entities, certain individuals, and others.)
► See separate instructions for each line.   ► Keep a copy for your records.

EIN

OMB No. 1545-0003

Type or print clearly.

1 Legal name of entity (or individual) for whom the EIN is being requested

2 Trade name of business (if different from name on line 1) | 3 Executor, trustee, "care of" name

4a Mailing address (room, apt., suite no. and street, or P.O. box) | 5a Street address (if different) (Do not enter a P.O. box.)

4b City, state, and ZIP code | 5b City, state, and ZIP code

6 County and state where principal business is located

7a Name of principal officer, general partner, grantor, owner, or trustor | 7b SSN, ITIN, or EIN

8a **Type of entity** (check only one box)
☐ Sole proprietor (SSN) _____
☐ Partnership
☐ Corporation (enter form number to be filed) ► _____
☐ Personal service corp.
☐ Church or church-controlled organization
☐ Other nonprofit organization (specify) ► _____
☐ Other (specify) ►

☐ Estate (SSN of decedent) _____
☐ Plan administrator (SSN) _____
☐ Trust (SSN of grantor) _____
☐ National Guard   ☐ State/local government
☐ Farmers' cooperative   ☐ Federal government/military
☐ REMIC   ☐ Indian tribal governments/enterprises
Group Exemption Number (GEN) ► _____

8b If a corporation, name the state or foreign country (if applicable) where incorporated | State | Foreign country

9 **Reason for applying** (check only one box)
☐ Started new business (specify type) ► _____
☐ Hired employees (Check the box and see line 12.)
☐ Compliance with IRS withholding regulations
☐ Other (specify) ►
☐ Banking purpose (specify purpose) ► _____
☐ Changed type of organization (specify new type) ► _____
☐ Purchased going business
☐ Created a trust (specify type) ► _____
☐ Created a pension plan (specify type) ► _____

10 Date business started or acquired (month, day, year) | 11 Closing month of accounting year

12 First date wages or annuities were paid or will be paid (month, day, year). **Note:** If applicant is a withholding agent, enter date income will first be paid to nonresident alien. (month, day, year) . . . . ►

13 Highest number of employees expected in the next 12 months. **Note:** If the applicant does not expect to have any employees during the period, enter "-0-." . . . . ► | Agricultural | Household | Other

14 Check **one** box that best describes the principal activity of your business. ☐ Health care & social assistance ☐ Wholesale-agent/broker
☐ Construction ☐ Rental & leasing ☐ Transportation & warehousing ☐ Accommodation & food service ☐ Wholesale-other ☐ Retail
☐ Real estate ☐ Manufacturing ☐ Finance & insurance ☐ Other (specify)

15 Indicate principal line of merchandise sold; specific construction work done; products produced; or services provided.

16a Has the applicant ever applied for an employer identification number for this or any other business? . . . . ☐ Yes ☐ No
Note: If "Yes," please complete lines 16b and 16c.

16b If you checked "Yes" on line 16a, give applicant's legal name and trade name shown on prior application if different from line 1 or 2 above.
Legal name ► | Trade name ►

16c Approximate date when, and city and state where, the application was filed. Enter previous employer identification number if known.
Approximate date when filed (mo., day, year) | City and state where filed | Previous EIN

Third Party Designee
Complete this section **only** if you want to authorize the named individual to receive the entity's EIN and answer questions about the completion of this form.
Designee's name | Designee's telephone number (include area code) (   )
Address and ZIP code | Designee's fax number (include area code) (   )

Under penalties of perjury, I declare that I have examined this application, and to the best of my knowledge and belief, it is true, correct, and complete.

Name and title (type or print clearly) ►

Signature ► | Date ►

Applicant's telephone number (include area code) (   )
Applicant's fax number (include area code) (   )

For Privacy Act and Paperwork Reduction Act Notice, see separate instructions.   Cat. No. 16055N   Form **SS-4** (Rev. 12-2001)

Do I Need an EIN?

File Form SS-4 if the applicant entity does not already have an EIN but is required to show an EIN on any return, statement, or other document.[1] **See also the separate instructions for each line on Form SS-4.**

IF the applicant...	AND...	THEN...
Started a new business	Does not currently have (nor expect to have) employees	Complete lines 1, 2, 4a–6, 8a, and 9–16c.
Hired (or will hire) employees, including household employees	Does not already have an EIN	Complete lines 1, 2, 4a–6, 7a–b (if applicable), 8a, 8b (if applicable), and 9–16c.
Opened a bank account	Needs an EIN for banking purposes only	Complete lines 1–5b, 7a–b (if applicable), 8a, 9, and 16a–c.
Changed type of organization	Either the legal character of the organization or its ownership changed (e.g., you incorporate a sole proprietorship or form a partnership)[2]	Complete lines 1–16c (as applicable).
Purchased a going business[3]	Does not already have an EIN	Complete lines 1–16c (as applicable).
Created a trust	The trust is other than a grantor trust or an IRA trust[4]	Complete lines 1–16c (as applicable).
Created a pension plan as a plan administrator[5]	Needs an EIN for reporting purposes	Complete lines 1, 2, 4a–6, 8a, 9, and 16a–c.
Is a foreign person needing an EIN to comply with IRS withholding regulations	Needs an EIN to complete a Form W-8 (other than Form W-8ECI), avoid withholding on portfolio assets, or claim tax treaty benefits[6]	Complete lines 1–5b, 7a–b (SSN or ITIN optional), 8a–9, and 16a–c.
Is administering an estate	Needs an EIN to report estate income on Form 1041	Complete lines 1, 3, 4a–b, 8a, 9, and 16a–c.
Is a withholding agent for taxes on non-wage income paid to an alien (i.e., individual, corporation, or partnership, etc.)	Is an agent, broker, fiduciary, manager, tenant, or spouse who is required to file **Form 1042,** Annual Withholding Tax Return for U.S. Source Income of Foreign Persons	Complete lines 1, 2, 3 (if applicable), 4a–5b, 7a–b (if applicable), 8a, 9, and 16a–c.
Is a state or local agency	Serves as a tax reporting agent for public assistance recipients under Rev. Proc. 80-4, 1980-1 C.B. 581[7]	Complete lines 1, 2, 4a–5b, 8a, 9, and 16a–c.
Is a single-member LLC	Needs an EIN to file **Form 8832,** Classification Election, for filing employment tax returns, **or** for state reporting purposes[8]	Complete lines 1–16c (as applicable).
Is an S corporation	Needs an EIN to file **Form 2553,** Election by a Small Business Corporation[9]	Complete lines 1–16c (as applicable).

[1] For example, a sole proprietorship or self-employed farmer who establishes a qualified retirement plan, or is required to file excise, employment, alcohol, tobacco, or firearms returns, must have an EIN. **A partnership, corporation, REMIC (real estate mortgage investment conduit), nonprofit organization (church, club, etc.), or farmers' cooperative must use an EIN for any tax-related purpose even if the entity does not have employees.**

[2] However, **do not** apply for a new EIN if the existing entity only **(a)** changed its business name, **(b)** elected on Form 8832 to change the way it is taxed (or is covered by the default rules), or **(c)** terminated its partnership status because at least 50% of the total interests in partnership capital and profits were sold or exchanged within a 12-month period. (The EIN of the terminated partnership should continue to be used. See Regulations section 301.6109-1(d)(2)(iii).)

[3] Do not use the EIN of the prior business unless you became the "owner" of a corporation by acquiring its stock.

[4] However, IRA trusts that are required to file **Form 990-T**, Exempt Organization Business Income Tax Return, must have an EIN.

[5] A plan administrator is the person or group of persons specified as the administrator by the instrument under which the plan is operated.

[6] Entities applying to be a Qualified Intermediary (QI) need a QI-EIN even if they already have an EIN. **See Rev. Proc. 2000-12.**

[7] See also Household employer on page 4. **(Note:** State or local agencies may need an EIN for other reasons, e.g., hired employees.)

[8] Most LLCs **do not** need to file Form 8832. See **Limited liability company (LLC)** on page 4 for details on completing Form SS-4 for an LLC.

[9] An existing corporation that is electing or revoking S corporation status should use its previously-assigned EIN.

※

Instructions for Form SS-4
(Rev. September 2003)

Department of the Treasury
Internal Revenue Service

For use with Form SS-4 (Rev. December 2001)
Application for Employer Identification Number.
Section references are to the Internal Revenue Code unless otherwise noted.

General Instructions

Use these instructions to complete **Form SS-4**, Application for Employer Identification Number. Also see **Do I Need an EIN?** on page 2 of Form SS-4.

Purpose of Form

Use Form SS-4 to apply for an employer identification number (EIN). An EIN is a nine-digit number (for example, 12-3456789) assigned to sole proprietors, corporations, partnerships, estates, trusts, and other entities for tax filing and reporting purposes. The information you provide on this form will establish your business tax account.

*An EIN is for use in connection with your business activities only. Do **not** use your EIN in place of your social security number (SSN).*

Items To Note

Apply online. You can now apply for and receive an EIN online using the internet. See **How To Apply** below.

File only one Form SS-4. Generally, a sole proprietor should file only one Form SS-4 and needs only one EIN, regardless of the number of businesses operated as a sole proprietorship or trade names under which a business operates. However, if the proprietorship incorporates or enters into a partnership, a new EIN is required. Also, each corporation in an affiliated group must have its own EIN.

EIN applied for, but not received. If you do not have an EIN by the time a return is due, write "Applied For" and the date you applied in the space shown for the number. **Do not** show your SSN as an EIN on returns.

If you do not have an EIN by the time a tax deposit is due, send your payment to the Internal Revenue Service Center for your filing area as shown in the instructions for the form that you are filing. Make your check or money order payable to the "United States Treasury" and show your name (as shown on Form SS-4), address, type of tax, period covered, and date you applied for an EIN.

How To Apply

You can apply for an EIN online, by telephone, by fax, or by mail depending on how soon you need to use the EIN. Use only one method for each entity so you do not receive more than one EIN for an entity.

Online. You can receive your EIN by internet and use it immediately to file a return or make a payment. Go to the

IRS website at **www.irs.gov/businesses** and click on **Employer ID Numbers** under **topics**.

Telephone. You can receive your EIN by telephone and use it immediately to file a return or make a payment. Call the IRS at **1-800-829-4933.** (International applicants must call 215-516-6999.) The hours of operation are 7:00 a.m. to 10:00 p.m. The person making the call must be authorized to sign the form or be an authorized designee. See **Signature** and **Third Party Designee** on page 6. Also see the **TIP** below.

If you are applying by telephone, it will be helpful to complete Form SS-4 before contacting the IRS. An IRS representative will use the information from the Form SS-4 to establish your account and assign you an EIN. Write the number you are given on the upper right corner of the form and sign and date it. Keep this copy for your records.

If requested by an IRS representative, mail or fax (facsimile) the signed Form SS-4 (including any Third Party Designee authorization) within 24 hours to the IRS address provided by the IRS representative.

*Taxpayer representatives can apply for an EIN on behalf of their client and request that the EIN be faxed to their **client** on the same day. Note: By using this procedure, you are authorizing the IRS to fax the EIN without a cover sheet.*

Fax. Under the Fax-TIN program, you can receive your EIN by fax within 4 business days. Complete and fax Form SS-4 to the IRS using the Fax-TIN number listed on page 2 for your state. A long-distance charge to callers outside of the local calling area will apply. Fax-TIN numbers can only be used to apply for an EIN. **The numbers may change without notice.** Fax-TIN is available 24 hours a day, 7 days a week.

Be sure to provide your fax number so the IRS can fax the EIN back to you. Note: By using this procedure, you are authorizing the IRS to fax the EIN without a cover sheet.

Mail. Complete Form SS-4 at least 4 to 5 weeks before you will need an EIN. Sign and date the application and mail it to the service center address for your state. You will receive your EIN in the mail in approximately 4 weeks. See also **Third Party Designee** on page 6.

Call 1-800-829-4933 to verify a number or to ask about the status of an application by mail.

Cat. No. 62736F

Where To Fax or File

If your principal business, office or agency, or legal residence in the case of an individual, is located in:	Call the Fax-TIN number shown or file with the "Internal Revenue Service Center" at:
Connecticut, Delaware, District of Columbia, Florida, Georgia, Maine, Maryland, Massachusetts, New Hampshire, New Jersey, New York, North Carolina, Ohio, Pennsylvania, Rhode Island, South Carolina, Vermont, Virginia, West Virginia	Attn: EIN Operation P. 0. Box 9003 Holtsville, NY 11742-9003 Fax-TIN 631-447-8960
Illinois, Indiana, Kentucky, Michigan	Attn: EIN Operation Cincinnati, OH 45999 Fax-TIN 859-669-5760
Alabama, Alaska, Arizona, Arkansas, California, Colorado, Hawaii, Idaho, Iowa, Kansas, Louisiana, Minnesota, Mississippi, Missouri, Montana, Nebraska, Nevada, New Mexico, North Dakota, Oklahoma, Oregon, Puerto Rico, South Dakota, Tennessee, Texas, Utah, Washington, Wisconsin, Wyoming	Attn: EIN Operation Philadelphia, PA 19255 Fax-TIN 215-516-3990
If you have no legal residence, principal place of business, or principal office or agency in any state:	Attn: EIN Operation Philadelphia, PA 19255 Telephone 215-516-6999 Fax-TIN 215-516-3990

How To Get Forms and Publications

Phone. You can order forms, instructions, and publications by phone 24 hours a day, 7 days a week. Call 1-800-TAX-FORM (1-800-829-3676). You should receive your order or notification of its status within 10 workdays.

Personal computer. With your personal computer and modem, you can get the forms and information you need using the IRS website at **www.irs.gov** or File Transfer Protocol at **ftp.irs.gov**.

CD-ROM. For small businesses, return preparers, or others who may frequently need tax forms or publications, a CD-ROM containing over 2,000 tax products (including many prior year forms) can be purchased from the National Technical Information Service (NTIS).

To order **Pub. 1796**, Federal Tax Products on CD-ROM, call **1-877-CDFORMS** (1-877-233-6767) toll free or connect to **www.irs.gov/cdorders**.

Tax Help for Your Business

IRS-sponsored Small Business Workshops provide information about your Federal and state tax obligations.

For information about workshops in your area, call 1-800-829-4933.

Related Forms and Publications

The following **forms** and **instructions** may be useful to filers of Form SS-4:
- **Form 990-T**, Exempt Organization Business Income Tax Return
- **Instructions for Form 990-T**
- **Schedule C (Form 1040)**, Profit or Loss From Business
- **Schedule F (Form 1040)**, Profit or Loss From Farming
- **Instructions for Form 1041 and Schedules A, B, D, G, I, J, and K-1**, U.S. Income Tax Return for Estates and Trusts
- **Form 1042**, Annual Withholding Tax Return for U.S. Source Income of Foreign Persons
- **Instructions for Form 1065**, U.S. Return of Partnership Income
- **Instructions for Form 1066**, U.S. Real Estate Mortgage Investment Conduit (REMIC) Income Tax Return
- **Instructions for Forms 1120 and 1120-A**
- **Form 2553**, Election by a Small Business Corporation
- **Form 2848**, Power of Attorney and Declaration of Representative
- **Form 8821**, Tax Information Authorization
- **Form 8832**, Entity Classification Election
  For more **information** about filing Form SS-4 and related issues, see:
- **Circular A**, Agricultural Employer's Tax Guide (Pub. 51)
- **Circular E**, Employer's Tax Guide (Pub. 15)
- **Pub. 538**, Accounting Periods and Methods
- **Pub. 542**, Corporations
- **Pub. 557**, Exempt Status for Your Organization
- **Pub. 583**, Starting a Business and Keeping Records
- **Pub. 966**, Electronic Choices for Paying ALL Your Federal Taxes
- **Pub. 1635**, Understanding Your EIN
- **Package 1023**, Application for Recognition of Exemption Under Section 501(c)(3) of the Internal Revenue Code
- **Package 1024**, Application for Recognition of Exemption Under Section 501(a)

Specific Instructions

Print or type all entries on Form SS-4. Follow the instructions for each line to expedite processing and to avoid unnecessary IRS requests for additional information. Enter "N/A" (nonapplicable) on the lines that do not apply.

Line 1—Legal name of entity (or individual) for whom the EIN is being requested. Enter the legal name of the entity (or individual) applying for the EIN exactly as it appears on the social security card, charter, or other applicable legal document.

Individuals. Enter your first name, middle initial, and last name. If you are a sole proprietor, enter your individual name, not your business name. Enter your business name on line 2. Do not use abbreviations or nicknames on line 1.

Trusts. Enter the name of the trust.

Estate of a decedent. Enter the name of the estate.

Partnerships. Enter the legal name of the partnership as it appears in the partnership agreement.

Corporations. Enter the corporate name as it appears in the corporation charter or other legal document creating it.

Plan administrators. Enter the name of the plan administrator. A plan administrator who already has an EIN should use that number.

Line 2—Trade name of business. Enter the trade name of the business if different from the legal name. The trade name is the "doing business as " (DBA) name.

 *Use the full legal name shown on line 1 on all tax returns filed for the entity. (However, if you enter a trade name on line 2 and choose to use the trade name instead of the legal name, enter the trade name on **all returns** you file.) To prevent processing delays and errors, **always** use the legal name only (or the trade name only) on **all** tax returns.*

Line 3—Executor, trustee, "care of" name. Trusts enter the name of the trustee. Estates enter the name of the executor, administrator, or other fiduciary. If the entity applying has a designated person to receive tax information, enter that person's name as the "care of" person. Enter the individual's first name, middle initial, and last name.

Lines 4a-b—Mailing address. Enter the mailing address for the entity's correspondence. If line 3 is completed, enter the address for the executor, trustee or "care of" person. Generally, this address will be used on all tax returns.

 *File **Form 8822**, Change of Address, to report any subsequent changes to the entity's mailing address.*

Lines 5a-b—Street address. Provide the entity's physical address **only** if different from its mailing address shown in lines 4a-b. **Do not** enter a P.O. box number here.

Line 6—County and state where principal business is located. Enter the entity's primary **physical** location.

Lines 7a-b—Name of principal officer, general partner, grantor, owner, or trustor. Enter the first name, middle initial, last name, and SSN of **(a)** the principal officer if the business is a corporation, **(b)** a general partner if a partnership, **(c)** the owner of an entity that is disregarded as separate from its owner (disregarded entities owned by a corporation enter the corporation's name and EIN), or **(d)** a grantor, owner, or trustor if a trust.

If the person in question is an **alien individual** with a previously assigned individual taxpayer identification number (ITIN), enter the ITIN in the space provided and submit a copy of an official identifying document. If

necessary, complete **Form W-7,** Application for IRS Individual Taxpayer Identification Number, to obtain an ITIN.

You are **required** to enter an SSN, ITIN, or EIN unless the only reason you are applying for an EIN is to make an entity classification election (see Regulations sections 301.7701-1 through 301.7701-3) and you are a nonresident alien with no effectively connected income from sources within the United States.

Line 8a—Type of entity. Check the box that best describes the type of entity applying for the EIN. If you are an alien individual with an ITIN previously assigned to you, enter the ITIN in place of a requested SSN.

 *This is not an election for a tax classification of an entity. See **Limited liability company** (LLC) on page 4.*

Other. If not specifically listed, check the "Other" box, enter the type of entity and the type of return, if any, that will be filed (for example, "Common Trust Fund, Form 1065" or "Created a Pension Plan"). Do not enter "N/A." If you are an alien individual applying for an EIN, see the **Lines 7a-b** instructions above.

● **Household employer.** If you are an individual, check the "Other" box and enter "Household Employer" and your SSN. If you are a state or local agency serving as a tax reporting agent for public assistance recipients who become household employers, check the "Other" box and enter "Household Employer Agent." If you are a trust that qualifies as a household employer, you do not need a separate EIN for reporting tax information relating to household employees; use the EIN of the trust.

● **QSub.** For a qualified subchapter S subsidiary (QSub) check the "Other" box and specify "QSub."

● **Withholding agent.** If you are a withholding agent required to file Form 1042, check the "Other" box and enter "Withholding Agent."

Sole proprietor. Check this box if you file Schedule C, C-EZ, or F (Form 1040) and have a qualified plan, or are required to file excise, employment, alcohol, tobacco, or firearms returns, or are a payer of gambling winnings. Enter your SSN (or ITIN) in the space provided. If you are a nonresident alien with no effectively connected income from sources within the United States, you do not need to enter an SSN or ITIN.

Corporation. This box is for any corporation **other** than a personal service corporation. If you check this box, enter the income tax form number to be filed by the entity in the space provided.

 *If you entered "1120S" after the "Corporation" checkbox, the corporation **must** file Form 2553 no later than the 15th day of the 3rd month of the tax year the election is to take effect. Until Form 2553 has been received and approved, you will be considered a Form 1120 filer. See the Instructions for Form 2553.*

Personal service corp. Check this box if the entity is a personal service corporation. An entity is a personal service corporation for a tax year only if:

- The principal activity of the entity during the testing period (prior tax year) for the tax year is the performance of personal services substantially by employee-owners, and
- The employee-owners own at least 10% of the fair market value of the outstanding stock in the entity on the last day of the testing period.

Personal services include performance of services in such fields as health, law, accounting, or consulting. For more information about personal service corporations, see the Instructions for Forms 1120 and 1120-A and Pub. 542.

Other nonprofit organization. Check this box if the nonprofit organization is other than a church or church-controlled organization and specify the type of nonprofit organization (for example, an educational organization).

 *If the organization also seeks tax-exempt status, you **must** file either Package 1023 or Package 1024. See Pub. 557 for more information.*

If the organization is covered by a group exemption letter, enter the four-digit **group exemption number (GEN).** (Do not confuse the GEN with the nine-digit EIN.) If you do not know the GEN, contact the parent organization. Get Pub. 557 for more information about group exemption numbers.

Plan administrator. If the plan administrator is an individual, enter the plan administrator's SSN in the space provided.

REMIC. Check this box if the entity has elected to be treated as a real estate mortgage investment conduit (REMIC). See the Instructions for Form 1066 for more information.

Limited liability company (LLC). An LLC is an entity organized under the laws of a state or foreign country as a limited liability company. For Federal tax purposes, an LLC may be treated as a partnership or corporation or be disregarded as an entity separate from its owner.

By **default,** a domestic LLC with only one member is **disregarded** as an entity separate from its owner and must include all of its income and expenses on the owner's tax return (e.g., **Schedule C (Form 1040)**). Also by default, a domestic LLC with two or more members is treated as a partnership. A domestic LLC may file Form 8832 to avoid either default classification and elect to be classified as an association taxable as a corporation. For more information on entity classifications (including the rules for foreign entities), see the instructions for Form 8832.

 Do not** file Form 8832 if the LLC accepts the default classifications above. **However, if the LLC will be electing S Corporation status, it must timely file both Form 8832 and Form 2553.

Complete Form SS-4 for LLCs as follows:
- A single-member domestic LLC that accepts the default classification (above) does not need an EIN and generally should not file Form SS-4. Generally, the LLC

should use the name and EIN of its **owner** for all Federal tax purposes. However, the reporting and payment of employment taxes for employees of the LLC may be made using the name and EIN of **either** the owner or the LLC as explained in Notice 99-6. You can find Notice 99-6 on page 12 of Internal Revenue Bulletin 1999-3 at **www.irs.gov/pub/irs-irbs/irb99-03.pdf. (Note:** If the LLC applicant indicates in box 13 that it has employees or expects to have employees, the owner (whether an individual or other entity) of a single-member domestic LLC will also be assigned its own EIN (if it does not already have one) even if the LLC will be filing the employment tax returns.)
- A single-member, domestic LLC that accepts the default classification (above) and wants an EIN for filing employment tax returns (see above) or non-Federal purposes, such as a state requirement, must check the "Other" box and write "Disregarded Entity" or, when applicable, "Disregarded Entity—Sole Proprietorship" in the space provided.
- A multi-member, domestic LLC that accepts the default classification (above) must check the "Partnership" box.
- A domestic LLC that will be filing Form 8832 to elect corporate status must check the "Corporation" box and write in "Single-Member" or "Multi-Member" immediately below the "form number" entry line.

Line 9—Reason for applying. Check only **one** box. Do not enter "N/A."

Started new business. Check this box if you are starting a new business that requires an EIN. If you check this box, enter the type of business being started. **Do not** apply if you already have an EIN and are only adding another place of business.

Hired employees. Check this box if the existing business is requesting an EIN because it has hired or is hiring employees and is therefore required to file employment tax returns. **Do not** apply if you already have an EIN and are only hiring employees. For information on employment taxes (e.g., for family members), see Circular E.

 You may be required to make electronic deposits of all depository taxes (such as employment tax, excise tax, and corporate income tax) using the Electronic Federal Tax Payment System (EFTPS). See section 11, Depositing Taxes, of Circular E and Pub. 966.

Created a pension plan. Check this box if you have created a pension plan and need an EIN for reporting purposes. Also, enter the type of plan in the space provided.

 Check this box if you are applying for a trust EIN when a new pension plan is established. In addition, check the "Other" box in line 8a and write "Created a Pension Plan" in the space provided.

Banking purpose. Check this box if you are requesting an EIN for banking purposes only, and enter the banking purpose (for example, a bowling league for depositing dues or an investment club for dividend and interest reporting).

Changed type of organization. Check this box if the business is changing its type of organization. For example, the business was a sole proprietorship and has been incorporated or has become a partnership. If you check this box, specify in the space provided (including available space immediately below) the type of change made. For example, "From Sole Proprietorship to Partnership."

Purchased going business. Check this box if you purchased an existing business. **Do not** use the former owner's EIN unless you became the "owner" of a corporation by acquiring its stock.

Created a trust. Check this box if you created a trust, and enter the type of trust created. For example, indicate if the trust is a nonexempt charitable trust or a split-interest trust.

Exception. Do **not** file this form for certain grantor-type trusts. The trustee does not need an EIN for the trust if the trustee furnishes the name and TIN of the grantor/owner and the address of the trust to all payors. See the Instructions for Form 1041 for more information.

 Do not check this box if you are applying for a trust EIN when a new pension plan is established. Check "Created a pension plan."

Other. Check this box if you are requesting an EIN for any other reason; and enter the reason. For example, a newly-formed state government entity should enter "Newly-Formed State Government Entity" in the space provided.

Line 10—Date business started or acquired. If you are starting a new business, enter the starting date of the business. If the business you acquired is already operating, enter the date you acquired the business. If you are changing the form of ownership of your business, enter the date the new ownership entity began. Trusts should enter the date the trust was legally created. Estates should enter the date of death of the decedent whose name appears on line 1 or the date when the estate was legally funded.

Line 11—Closing month of accounting year. Enter the last month of your accounting year or tax year. An accounting or tax year is usually 12 consecutive months, either a calendar year or a fiscal year (including a period of 52 or 53 weeks). A calendar year is 12 consecutive months ending on December 31. A fiscal year is either 12 consecutive months ending on the last day of any month other than December or a 52-53 week year. For more information on accounting periods, see Pub. 538.

Individuals. Your tax year generally will be a calendar year.

Partnerships. Partnerships must adopt one of the following tax years:
• The tax year of the majority of its partners,
• The tax year common to all of its principal partners,
• The tax year that results in the least aggregate deferral of income, or
• In certain cases, some other tax year.

See the Instructions for Form 1065 for more information.

REMICs. REMICs must have a calendar year as their tax year.

Personal service corporations. A personal service corporation generally must adopt a calendar year unless:
• It can establish a business purpose for having a different tax year, or
• It elects under section 444 to have a tax year other than a calendar year.

Trusts. Generally, a trust must adopt a calendar year except for the following:
• Tax-exempt trusts,
• Charitable trusts, and
• Grantor-owned trusts.

Line 12—First date wages or annuities were paid or will be paid. If the business has or will have employees, enter the date on which the business began or will begin to pay wages. If the business does not plan to have employees, enter "N/A."

Withholding agent. Enter the date you began or will begin to pay income (including annuities) to a nonresident alien. This also applies to individuals who are required to file Form 1042 to report alimony paid to a nonresident alien.

Line 13—Highest number of employees expected in the next 12 months. Complete each box by entering the number (including zero ("-0-")) of "Agricultural," "Household," or "Other" employees expected by the applicant in the next 12 months. For a definition of agricultural labor (farmwork), see Circular A.

Lines 14 and 15. Check the **one** box in line 14 that best describes the principal activity of the applicant's business. Check the "Other" box (and specify the applicant's principal activity) if none of the listed boxes applies.

Use line 15 to describe the applicant's principal line of business in more detail. For example, if you checked the "Construction" box in line 14, enter additional detail such as "General contractor for residential buildings" in line 15.

Construction. Check this box if the applicant is engaged in erecting buildings or other structures, (e.g., streets, highways, bridges, tunnels). The term "Construction" also includes special trade contractors, (e.g., plumbing, HVAC, electrical, carpentry, concrete, excavation, etc. contractors).

Real estate. Check this box if the applicant is engaged in renting or leasing real estate to others; managing, selling, buying or renting real estate for others; or providing related real estate services (e.g., appraisal services).

Rental and leasing. Check this box if the applicant is engaged in providing tangible goods such as autos, computers, consumer goods, or industrial machinery and equipment to customers in return for a periodic rental or lease payment.

Manufacturing. Check this box if the applicant is engaged in the mechanical, physical, or chemical transformation of materials, substances, or components into new products. The assembling of component parts of manufactured products is also considered to be manufacturing.

Transportation & warehousing. Check this box if the applicant provides transportation of passengers or cargo; warehousing or storage of goods; scenic or sight-seeing transportation; or support activities related to these modes of transportation.

Finance & insurance. Check this box if the applicant is engaged in transactions involving the creation, liquidation, or change of ownership of financial assets and/or facilitating such financial transactions; underwriting annuities/insurance policies; facilitating such underwriting by selling insurance policies; or by providing other insurance or employee-benefit related services.

Health care and social assistance. Check this box if the applicant is engaged in providing physical, medical, or psychiatric care using licensed health care professionals or providing social assistance activities such as youth centers, adoption agencies, individual/family services, temporary shelters, etc.

Accommodation & food services. Check this box if the applicant is engaged in providing customers with lodging, meal preparation, snacks, or beverages for immediate consumption.

Wholesale–agent/broker. Check this box if the applicant is engaged in arranging for the purchase or sale of goods owned by others or purchasing goods on a commission basis for goods traded in the wholesale market, usually between businesses.

Wholesale–other. Check this box if the applicant is engaged in selling goods in the wholesale market generally to other businesses for resale on their own account.

Retail. Check this box if the applicant is engaged in selling merchandise to the general public from a fixed store; by direct, mail-order, or electronic sales; or by using vending machines.

Other. Check this box if the applicant is engaged in an activity not described above. Describe the applicant's principal business activity in the space provided.

Lines 16a-c. Check the applicable box in line 16a to indicate whether or not the entity (or individual) applying for an EIN was issued one previously. Complete lines 16b and 16c **only** if the "Yes" box in line 16a is checked. If the applicant previously applied for **more than one** EIN, write "See Attached" in the empty space in line 16a and attach a separate sheet providing the line 16b and 16c information for each EIN previously requested.

Third Party Designee. Complete this section **only** if you want to authorize the named individual to receive the entity's EIN and answer questions about the completion of Form SS-4. The designee's authority terminates at the time the EIN is assigned and released to the designee. **You must complete the signature area for the authorization to be valid.**

Signature. When required, the application must be signed by **(a)** the individual, if the applicant is an individual, **(b)** the president, vice president, or other principal officer, if the applicant is a corporation, **(c)** a responsible and duly authorized member or officer having knowledge of its affairs, if the applicant is a partnership, government entity, or other unincorporated organization, or **(d)** the fiduciary, if the applicant is a trust or an estate. Foreign applicants may have any duly-authorized person, (e.g., division manager), sign Form SS-4.

Privacy Act and Paperwork Reduction Act Notice. We ask for the information on this form to carry out the Internal Revenue laws of the United States. We need it to comply with section 6109 and the regulations thereunder which generally require the inclusion of an employer identification number (EIN) on certain returns, statements, or other documents filed with the Internal Revenue Service. If your entity is required to obtain an EIN, you are required to provide all of the information requested on this form. Information on this form may be used to determine which Federal tax returns you are required to file and to provide you with related forms and publications.

We disclose this form to the Social Security Administration for their use in determining compliance with applicable laws. We may give this information to the Department of Justice for use in civil and criminal litigation, and to the cities, states, and the District of Columbia for use in administering their tax laws. We may also disclose this information to Federal and state agencies to enforce Federal nontax criminal laws and to combat terrorism.

We will be unable to issue an EIN to you unless you provide all of the requested information which applies to your entity. Providing false information could subject you to penalties.

You are not required to provide the information requested on a form that is subject to the Paperwork Reduction Act unless the form displays a valid OMB control number. Books or records relating to a form or its instructions must be retained as long as their contents may become material in the administration of any Internal Revenue law. Generally, tax returns and return information are confidential, as required by section 6103.

The time needed to complete and file this form will vary depending on individual circumstances. The estimated average time is:

Recordkeeping	6 min.
Learning about the law or the form	22 min.
Preparing the form	46 min.
Copying, assembling, and sending the form to the IRS	20 min.

If you have comments concerning the accuracy of these time estimates or suggestions for making this form simpler, we would be happy to hear from you. You can write to the Tax Products Coordinating Committee, Western Area Distribution Center, Rancho Cordova, CA 95743-0001. **Do not** send the form to this address. Instead, see **How To Apply** on page 1.

Copyright
United States Copyright Office

Copyright Registration for Musical Compositions

General Information

The copyright law of the United States provides for copyright protection in "musical works, including any accompanying words," which are fixed in some tangible medium of expression. 17 U.S.C. § 102(a)(2). Musical works include both original compositions and original arrangements or other new versions of earlier compositions to which new copyrightable authorship has been added.

The owner of copyright in a work has the exclusive right to make copies, to prepare derivative works, to sell or distribute copies, and to perform the work publicly. Anyone else wishing to use the work in these ways must have the permission of the author or someone who has derived rights through the author.

NOTE: Copyright in a musical work includes the right to make and distribute the first sound recording. Although others are permitted to make subsequent sound recordings, they must compensate the copyright owner of the musical work under the compulsory licensing provision of the law (17 U.S.C. § 115). For more information, please request Circular 73, *Compulsory License for Making and Distributing Phonorecords.*

Copyright Protection Is Automatic

Under the present copyright law, which became effective Jan. 1, 1978, a work is automatically protected by copyright when it is created. A work is created when it is "fixed" in a copy or phonorecord for the first time. Neither registration in the Copyright Office nor publication is required for copyright protection under the present law.

Advantages to Copyright Registration

There are, however, certain advantages to registration, including the establishment of a public record of the copyright claim. Copyright registration must generally be made before an infringement suit may be brought. Timely registration may also provide a broader range of remedies in an infringement suit.

Publication

Publication, as defined by the Copyright Act, is the distribution of copies or phonorecords of a work to the public by sale or other transfer of ownership, or by rental, lease, or lending. The offering to distribute copies or phonorecords to a group of persons for purposes of further distribution, public performance, or public display, constitutes publication. A public performance or display of a work does not of itself constitute publication.

Copyright Registration for Musical Compositions

"To the public" generally means to persons under no explicit or implicit restrictions with respect to disclosure. The following acts do *not* constitute publication: performance of the work, preparation of copies or phonorecords, or sending the work to the Copyright Office.

The above definition of publication applies *only* to works governed by the copyright law that took effect Jan. 1, 1978. For information about works published prior to 1978, call the Copyright Office at (202) 707-3000. Recorded information is available 24 hours a day, 7 days a week. Information specialists are on duty from 8:30 a.m. to 5 p.m., eastern time, Monday through Friday, except federal holidays. The TTY number is (202) 707-6737.

Registration Procedures

If you choose to register a claim in your work, package together the following material in the same envelope:

1 A properly completed application form;

2 A nonreturnable deposit of the work to be registered; and

3 A nonrefundable filing fee of $30* in the form of a check or money order payable to *Register of Copyrights* with each application.

Send the items to:

> Library of Congress
> Copyright Office
> 101 Independence Avenue, S.E.
> Washington, D.C. 20559-6000

*NOTE: Copyright Office fees are subject to change. For current fees, please check the Copyright Office website at *www.copyright.gov*, write the Copyright Office, or call (202) 707-3000.

Application Form

Form PA *is the appropriate form for registration, whether it is accompanied by the deposit of a "copy" (lead sheet or sheet music) or a "phonorecord" (disk or tape).* The form should be completed with black ink or type. Do not use pencil or send a carbon copy. All pertinent information should be supplied on the basic application form. A Continuation Sheet supplied by the Copyright Office should be used only when all necessary information cannot be recorded on the basic application form. No other attachments will be accepted.

Short Form PA may be used instead of Form PA in certain circumstances to register published and unpublished works of the performing arts, including dramas, music, and lyrics. Audiovisual works, including motion pictures, must be registered on the standard forms.

Who May Use the Short Forms

1 Any living author who is the only author of his or her work. Groups of authors or business organizations must use the standard forms.

2 An author who is the sole owner of the copyright in the work.

Other Requirements for Using the Short Forms

1 The work must be completely new in the sense that it does not contain substantial material that has been previously published or registered or that is in the public domain.

2 The work must *not* be a work made for hire. That is, the work must *not* be prepared by an employee within the scope of his or her employment or be a work specially ordered or commissioned for use as a contribution to a collective work.

Short Form PA is not appropriate for an anonymous author who does not want to reveal his or her identity.

Form SR is for registration of "sound recordings," which are works that result from the fixation of a series of sounds. The author of a sound recording is the performer, or the record producer, or both. Form SR may be used to register both a musical work and a sound recording fixed in a phonorecord, provided that the same person or organization owns the copyrights in both works. If both kinds of work are being registered, Space 2 of Form SR must clearly account for the authorship of both the musical composition (music or words and music) and the sound recording (performance, sound recording, or both). Request Circular 56, *Copyright Registration for Sound Recordings*, for detailed information about the registration of claims in sound recordings.

How to Complete Form PA

Instructions for completing each space of the application accompany the form. Nevertheless, registration is often delayed because of mistakes in filling out the form. The following points should be noted in particular:

Space 1: Title. Give the title of the work exactly as it appears on the copy or phonorecord.

- A group of *unpublished* works registered as a collection must be given a collection title. The individual titles may be given on a Continuation Sheet.

- For registration of an entire collection of *published* works, give the title of the collection.

- For registration of only some of the individual works in a published collection, give the titles of the individual works, followed by "Contained in (title of collection)."

See the section in this circular under "Collections of Music" (p. 5) for further information.

Space 2: Author. Answer carefully the question "Was this author's contribution to the work a 'work made for hire'?" Check "yes" *only* if that contribution was either (1) prepared by an employee within the scope of his or her employment or (2) specially ordered for a certain use, with an express written agreement signed by both parties that the work shall be considered a work made for hire. Such certain uses include contributions to a collective work, parts of a motion picture or other audiovisual work, or supplementary works, such as new musical arrangements. If the contribution was made for hire, give the name of the *employer*, not the person who actually did the writing, in the "Name of Author" box.

Complete the "Nature of Authorship" space to specify what the author created as written or recorded in the copy or phonorecord that accompanies the application. Examples are: "music," "words," "arrangement." Do *not* include elements not present in that copy or phonorecord. Do *not* include elements that are not protected by copyright, such as an idea, concept, name, or title.

Space 3: Year of Creation. The year of creation is the year in which the version of the work to be registered was *first* fixed in writing or recorded in any other tangible form. When a work is written or recorded over a period of time or constitutes a new version of an earlier work, give the completion date of the final work or new version. *This year date must always be given.*

First Publication. If publication has not taken place, *leave this part of Space 3 blank.* If the version of the work being registered has been published, give the month, day, year, and nation where copies or phonorecords of this version were first published.

Space 4: Claimant(s). The *name* and *address* of the *copyright claimant(s) must be given.* The copyright claimant is either the author or a person or organization to whom the author has transferred *all* the rights in the U.S. copyright. When the claimant named is *not* the author, a brief *transfer* statement

is required at Space 4 to show how the claimant acquired the copyright. Examples of generally acceptable statements include: "by written agreement"; "assignment"; "written contract"; and "by will." Do not attach copies of documents of copyright transfer to the application. For information on how to record transfers or other documents pertaining to a copyright, request Circular 12, *Recordation of Transfers and Other Documents.*

When the name of the claimant is not the name of the author given at Space 2 but the two names identify one person, the relationship between the names should be explained at Space 4. Examples are: "Doe Publishing Company, solely owned by John Doe" or "John Doe doing business as Doe Publishing Company."

Space 5: Previous Registration. If this work was not previously registered, answer "no" to the first question and *leave the rest of Space 5 blank.* If the work or part of the work was previously registered and a certificate of registration was issued, answer "yes" to the first question and check the appropriate box to show why another registration is sought. Also, give the requested information about the previous registration.

Space 6: Derivative Work or Compilation. Complete this space only if the work being registered contains a *substantial* amount of material:

1 that was previously published; or

2 that was previously registered in the United States Copyright Office; or

3 that is in the public domain; or

4 that for any reason is not part of this claim.

Leave this space blank if the work does not contain a substantial amount of any of these four kinds of material.

Space 6a: Preexisting Material. Briefly describe the preexisting material that has been used.

Space 6b: Material Added to this Work. Complete this space by stating briefly but clearly *all* the added or revised copyrightable material that forms the basis of the present registration. Examples: "Arrangement for piano and orchestra" or "new lyric."

Compilation of Musical Works

A "compilation" is a work formed by the collecting and assembling of preexisting materials that are selected, coordinated, or arranged in such a way that the resulting work as a whole constitutes an original work of authorship.

When an author contributes a certain minimum amount of authorship in the selection and ordering of *preexisting* musical compositions, the author creates a copyrightable compilation. The copyright in the compilation of the musical compositions is separate and distinct from copyright (if any) in the musical compositions themselves. Protection in the compilation extends *only* to the selection and ordering of the musical compositions.

For compilations, give a brief, general statement describing both the material that has been compiled *and* the compilation itself. Example: "Compilation of selected 19th century military songs."

In Space 2, use the same statement to describe the nature of the author's contribution.

Space 8: Certification. The application must bear an original signature and be dated. Stamped signatures are not acceptable. For a published work, the application must be certified on or after the date of first publication. If the certification date is earlier than the date of publication given at Space 3, the application cannot be accepted.

Deposit Requirements

The application must be accompanied by a deposit of the work to be registered. The deposit requirement varies according to the type of work for which registration is sought. Deposits cannot be returned.

Unpublished Works

Deposit one complete copy (lead sheet or sheet music) or phonorecord (disk or tape). "Complete" means that the deposit includes everything that is to be covered by the registration. Separate applications for several works may be accompanied by one phonorecord containing all the works. Registration generally covers only the material that is deposited for registration, even though the copyright law automatically gives copyright protection to all copyrightable authorship that is fixed in a copy or phonorecord.

Copies should be legible, and both words and music on a phonorecord should be clear and audible. All deposits should bear the title of the work.

Copies of a group of works registered as a collection should be assembled in orderly form and fastened together or placed in a folder. The title of a collection should appear on copies and phonorecords.

Published Works

For a musical work first published in the United States on or after Jan. 1, 1978, the deposit generally is two complete copies of the best edition.

Only one deposit is required for musical works that are:

- published only on phonorecords (tapes or disks), unless the claim includes the sound recording, in which case, two phonorecords are required as the deposit;

- published by rental, lease, or lending (Where there is a score and individual parts, only the score is required.);

- published as a single contribution to a collective work, for example, a hymn from a hymnal.

If first published in the United States *before Jan. 1, 1978*, the deposit is two complete copies of the best edition of the work as first published.

If first published outside the United States *before March 1, 1989*, the deposit is one complete copy or phonorecord of the work as first published.

For a musical work first published outside the United States *on or after March 1, 1989*, the deposit is either one complete copy or phonorecord of the work as first published or the best edition of the work.

For separate registration of a musical composition published only in a motion picture soundtrack, the deposit is:

1   One copy of the motion picture, or

2   Identifying material consisting of

  - a reproduction of the musical work, and

  - a sheet of paper containing the title of the motion picture and any credits or copyright notice for the musical work, if any.

"Best Edition" Requirements

The copyright law requires that copies or phonorecords deposited in the Copyright Office be of the "best edition" of the work. The law states, "The 'best edition' of a work is the edition, published in the United States at any time before the date of deposit, that the Library of Congress determines to be most suitable for its purposes." 17 U.S.C. § 101.

When two or more editions of the same version of a work have been published, the one of the highest quality is generally considered to be the best edition. In judging quality, the Library of Congress will adhere to the criteria set forth below in all but exceptional circumstances.

Copyright Registration for Musical Compositions

"Best Edition" of Published Copyrighted Musical Compositions

I   Printed Copies (rather than phonorecords)

  A   Fullness of Score
    1   Vocal music:
      a   With orchestral accompaniment—
        i   Full score and parts, if any, rather than conductor's score and parts, if any[1]
        ii   Conductor's score and parts, if any, rather than condensed score and parts, if any[2]
      b   Unaccompanied: Open score (each part on separate staff) rather than closed score (all parts condensed to two staffs)
    2   Instrumental music:
      a   Full score and parts, if any, rather than conductor's score and parts, if any[1]
      b   Conductor's score and parts, if any, rather than condensed score and parts, if any[2]

  B   Printing and Paper
    1   Archival-quality rather than less-permanent paper.

  C   Binding and Packaging
    1   Special limited editions rather than trade editions
    2   Bound rather than unbound
    3   If editions have different binding, apply the criteria in I.A.2–1.A.12, in Circular 7B, "Best Edition" of Published Copyrighted Works for the Collections of the Library of Congress.
    4   With protective folders rather than without

II   Phonorecords

  A   Compact digital disk rather than a vinyl disk

  B   Vinyl disk rather than tape

  C   With special enclosures rather than without

  D   Open-reel rather than cartridge

  E   Cartridge rather than cassette

  F   Quadraphonic rather than stereophonic

  G   True stereophonic rather than monaural

  H   Monaural rather than electronically rechanneled stereo

Collections of Music

Unpublished Collections

Two or more unpublished songs, song lyrics, or other musical works may be registered with one application and fee, *but only under certain conditions* stated in the Copyright Office regula-

tions. One of those conditions is that the copyright owner or owners must be the same for all the songs. Copyright belongs to the author and can be transferred only by a written agreement or other legal means. If there has been no transfer and the songs are by different authors, this copyright ownership requirement has not been met. An additional requirement is that there must always be at least one author common to all the songs, even if there has been a transfer of ownership.

In the following examples, the musical works *can be registered with one application*:

1   Al wrote the music and Sue wrote the lyrics to each of eight songs.
2   Sue wrote the music and Al and Larry wrote the lyrics to each of four songs.

In the following examples, the musical works *cannot be registered with one application*:

1   Al wrote the lyrics and music to three songs and co-wrote lyrics and music to four songs with Sue. (No transfer has taken place.)

2   Sue wrote the music for six songs; Al wrote the lyrics to two of the songs, and Larry wrote the lyrics to four of the songs.

Space 1 of the application should give a collection title. You may also give the individual titles. The collection title should also appear on the deposit copy or phonorecord.

Space 2 of the application should name all the individuals who contributed authorship to the musical works in the collection. If the authors are members of a performing group, you may state this after each name. Naming only a performing group as author does not clearly identify the authors.

When a group of unpublished works is registered as a collection, only the collection title will appear in the catalogs and indexes of the Copyright Office. Individual titles will appear in Copyright Office records only if each work is registered separately or if an application for supplementary registration is submitted to specify the individual titles in a collection. An application for supplementary registration may not be submitted until a certificate of registration has been issued for the collection. For more information on supplementary registration, please request Circular 8, *Supplementary Copyright Registration*, and application Form CA.

Published Collections

A published collection of musical compositions may be registered with one application and fee if all the compositions are owned by the same copyright claimant. The entire collection may be registered under the collection title.

Notice of Copyright

Before March 1, 1989, the use of copyright notice was mandatory on all published works, and any work first published before that date should have carried a notice. For works first published on and after March 1, 1989, use of the copyright notice is optional. For more information about copyright notice, see Circular 3, *Copyright Notice.*

Mandatory Deposit for Works Published in the United States

Although a copyright registration is not required, the Copyright Act establishes a mandatory deposit requirement for works published in the United States. In general, the owner of copyright or the owner of the exclusive right of publication in the work has a legal obligation to deposit in the Copyright Office within 3 months of publication in the United States *two* complete copies of the best edition. It is the responsibility of the owner of copyright or the owner of the right of first publication in the work to fulfill this mandatory deposit requirement. Failure to make the deposit can result in fines and other penalties but does not affect copyright protection.

Certain categories of works are *exempt entirely* from the mandatory deposit requirements, and the obligation is reduced for certain other categories. For further information, request Circular 7D, *Mandatory Deposit of Copies or Phonorecords for the Library of Congress.*

Effective Date of Registration

A copyright registration is effective on the date the Copyright Office receives all the required elements in acceptable form, regardless of how long it then takes to process the application and mail the certificate of registration. The time the Copyright Office requires to process an application varies, depending on the amount of material the Office is receiving.

If you apply for copyright registration, you will not receive an acknowledgment that your application has been received (the Office receives more than 600,000 applications annually), but you can expect

- A letter or a telephone call from a Copyright Office staff member if further information is needed or

- A certificate of registration indicating that the work has been registered, or if the application cannot be accepted, a letter explaining why it has been rejected.

If you want to know the date that the Copyright Office receives your material, send it by registered or certified mail and request a return receipt.

For Further Information

Information via the Internet

Frequently requested circulars, announcements, regulations, other related materials, and all copyright application forms are available via the Internet. You may access these from the Copyright Office website at *www.copyright.gov.*

Information by fax

Circulars and other information (but not application forms) are available by using a touchtone phone to access Fax-on-Demand at (202) 707-2600.

Information by telephone

For general information about copyright, call the Copyright Public Information Office at (202) 707-3000. The TTY number is (202) 707-6737. Information specialists are on duty from 8:30 a.m. to 5:00 p.m., eastern time, Monday through Friday, except federal holidays. Recorded information is available 24 hours a day. Or, if you know which application forms and circulars you want, request them 24 hours a day from the Forms and Publications Hotline at (202) 707-9100. Leave a recorded message.

Information by regular mail

Write to:
Library of Congress
Copyright Office
Publications Section, LM-455
101 Independence Avenue, S.E.
Washington, D.C. 20559-6000

Endnotes

1. In cases of compositions published only by rental, lease, or lending, this requirement is reduced to full score only.
2. In cases of compositions published only by rental, lease, or lending, this requirement is reduced to conductor's score only.

U.S. Copyright Office · The Library of Congress · 101 Independence Avenue, SE · Washington, DC 20559-6000 · www.copyright.gov

CIRCULAR 50   PRINT REV: 01/2004—30,000   WEB REV: 01/2004   Printed on recycled paper   U.S. GOVERNMENT PRINTING OFFICE: 2004-304-447/60,077

ⓒ Form PA

Detach and read these instructions before completing this form.
Make sure all applicable spaces have been filled in before you return this form.

When to Use This Form: Use Form PA for registration of published or unpublished works of the performing arts. This class includes works prepared for the purpose of being "performed" directly before an audience or indirectly "by means of any device or process." Works of the performing arts include: (1) musical works, including any accompanying words; (2) dramatic works, including any accompanying music; (3) pantomimes and choreographic works; and (4) motion pictures and other audiovisual works.

Deposit to Accompany Application: An application for copyright registration must be accompanied by a deposit consisting of copies or phonorecords representing the entire work for which registration is made. The following are the general deposit requirements as set forth in the statute:

Unpublished Work: Deposit one complete copy (or phonorecord).

Published Work: Deposit two complete copies (or one phonorecord) of the best edition.

Work First Published Outside the United States: Deposit one complete copy (or phonorecord) of the first foreign edition.

Contribution to a Collective Work: Deposit one complete copy (or phonorecord) of the best edition of the collective work.

Motion Pictures: Deposit *both* of the following: (1) a separate written description of the contents of the motion picture; and (2) for a published work, one complete copy of the best edition of the motion picture; or, for an unpublished work, one complete copy of the motion picture or identifying material. Identifying material may be either an audiorecording of the entire soundtrack or one frame enlargement or similar visual print from each 10-minute segment.

The Copyright Notice: Before March 1, 1989, the use of copyright notice was mandatory on all published works, and any work first published before that date should have carried a notice. For works first published on and after March 1, 1989, use of the copyright notice is optional. For more information about copyright notice, see Circular 3, "Copyright Notice."

For Further Information: To speak to an information specialist, call (202) 707-3000 (TTY: (202) 707-6737). Recorded information is available 24 hours a day. Order forms and other publications from the address in space 9 or call the Forms and Publications Hotline at (202) 707-9100. Most circulars (but not forms) are available via fax. Call (202) 707-2600 from a touchtone phone. Access and download circulars, forms, and other information from the Copyright Office website at *www.copyright.gov.*

PRIVACY ACT ADVISORY STATEMENT Required by the Privacy Act of 1974 (P.L. 93-579)
    The authority for requesting this information is title 17, U.S.C., secs. 409 and 410. Furnishing the requested information is voluntary. But if the information is not furnished, it may be necessary to delay or refuse registration and you may not be entitled to certain relief, remedies, and benefits provided in chapters 4 and 5 of title 17, U.S.C.
    The principal uses of the requested information are the establishment and maintenance of a public record and the examination of the application for compliance with the registration requirements of the copyright code.
    Other routine uses include public inspection and copying, preparation of public indexes, preparation of public catalogs of copyright registrations, and preparation of search reports upon request.
    NOTE: No other advisory statement will be given in connection with this application. Please keep this statement and refer to it if we communicate with you regarding this application.

Please type or print using black ink. The form is used to produce the certificate.

1 SPACE 1: Title

Title of This Work: Every work submitted for copyright registration must be given a title to identify that particular work. If the copies or phonorecords of the work bear a title (or an identifying phrase that could serve as a title), transcribe that wording *completely* and *exactly* on the application. Indexing of the registration and future identification of the work will depend on the information you give here. If the work you are registering is an entire "collective work" (such as a collection of plays or songs), give the overall title of the collection. If you are registering one or more individual contributions to a collective work, give the title of each contribution, followed by the title of the collection. For an unpublished collection, you may give the titles of the individual works after the collection title.

Previous or Alternative Titles: Complete this space if there are any additional titles for the work under which someone searching for the registration might be likely to look, or under which a document pertaining to the work might be recorded.

Nature of This Work: Briefly describe the general nature or character of the work being registered for copyright. Examples: "Music"; "Song Lyrics"; "Words and Music"; "Drama"; "Musical Play"; "Choreography"; "Pantomime"; "Motion Picture"; "Audiovisual Work."

2 SPACE 2: Author(s)

General Instructions: After reading these instructions, decide who are the "authors" of this work for copyright purposes. Then, unless the work is a "collective work," give the requested information about every "author" who contributed any appreciable amount of copyrightable matter to this version of the work. If you need further space, request additional Continuation Sheets. In the case of a collective work such as a songbook or a collection of plays, give information about the author of the collective work as a whole.

Name of Author: The fullest form of the author's name should be given. Unless the work was "made for hire," the individual who actually created the work is its "author." In the case of a work made for hire, the statute provides that "the employer or other person for whom the work was prepared is considered the author."

What is a "Work Made for Hire"? A "work made for hire" is defined as: (1) "a work prepared by an employee within the scope of his or her employment"; or (2) "a work specially ordered or commissioned for use as a contribution to a collective work, as a part of a motion picture or other audiovisual work, as a translation, as a

supplementary work, as a compilation, as an instructional text, as a test, as answer material for a test, or as an atlas, if the parties expressly agree in a written instrument signed by them that the work shall be considered a work made for hire." If you have checked "Yes" to indicate that the work was "made for hire," you must give the full legal name of the employer (or other person for whom the work was prepared). You may also include the name of the employee along with the name of the employer (for example: "Elster Music Co., employer for hire of John Ferguson").

"Anonymous" or "Pseudonymous" Work: An author's contribution to a work is "anonymous" if that author is not identified on the copies or phonorecords of the work. An author's contribution to a work is "pseudonymous" if that author is identified on the copies or phonorecords under a fictitious name. If the work is "anonymous" you may: (1) leave the line blank; or (2) state "anonymous" on the line; or (3) reveal the author's identity. If the work is "pseudonymous" you may: (1) leave the line blank; or (2) give the pseudonym and identify it as such (example: "Huntley Haverstock, pseudonym"); or (3) reveal the author's name, making clear which is the real name and which is the pseudonym (for example: "Judith Barton, whose pseudonym is Madeline Elster"). However, the citizenship or domicile of the author **must** be given in all cases.

Dates of Birth and Death: If the author is dead, the statute requires that the year of death be included in the application unless the work is anonymous or pseudonymous. The author's birth date is optional, but is useful as a form of identification. Leave this space blank if the author's contribution was a "work made for hire."

Author's Nationality or Domicile: Give the country of which the author is a citizen, or the country in which the author is domiciled. Nationality or domicile **must** be given in all cases.

Nature of Authorship: Give a brief general statement of the nature of this particular author's contribution to the work. Examples: "Words"; "Coauthor of Music"; "Words and Music"; "Arrangement"; "Coauthor of Book and Lyrics"; "Dramatization"; "Screen Play"; "Compilation and English Translation"; "Editorial Revisions."

3 SPACE 3: Creation and Publication

General Instructions: Do not confuse "creation" with "publication." Every application for copyright registration must state "the year in which creation of the work was completed." Give the date and nation of first publication only if the work has been published.

Creation: Under the statute, a work is "created" when it is fixed in a copy or phonorecord for the first time. Where a work has been prepared over a period of time, the part of the work existing in fixed form on a particular date constitutes the created work on that date. The date you give here should be the year in which the author completed the particular version for which registration is now being sought, even if other versions exist or if further changes or additions are planned.

Publication: The statute defines "publication" as "the distribution of copies or phonorecords of a work to the public by sale or other transfer of ownership, or by rental, lease, or lending"; a work is also "published" if there has been an "offering to distribute copies or phonorecords to a group of persons for purposes of further distribution, public performance, or public display." Give the full date (month, day, year) when, and the country where, publication first occurred. If first publication took place simultaneously in the United States and other countries, it is sufficient to state "U.S.A."

4 SPACE 4: Claimant(s)

Name(s) and Address(es) of Copyright Claimant(s): Give the name(s) and address(es) of the copyright claimant(s) in this work even if the claimant is the same as the author. Copyright in a work belongs initially to the author of the work (including, in the case of a work made for hire, the employer or other person for whom the work was prepared). The copyright claimant is either the author of the work or a person or organization to whom the copyright initially belonging to the author has been transferred.

Transfer: The statute provides that, if the copyright claimant is not the author, the application for registration must contain "a brief statement of how the claimant obtained ownership of the copyright." If any copyright claimant named in space 4 is not an author named in space 2, give a brief statement explaining how the claimant(s) obtained ownership of the copyright. Examples: "By written contract"; "Transfer of all rights by author"; "Assignment"; "By will." Do not attach transfer documents or other attachments or riders.

5 SPACE 5: Previous Registration

General Instructions: The questions in space 5 are intended to show whether an earlier registration has been made for this work and, if so, whether there is any basis for a new registration. As a general rule, only one basic copyright registration can be made for the same version of a particular work.

Same Version: If this version is substantially the same as the work covered by a previous registration, a second registration is not generally possible unless: (1) the work has been registered in unpublished form and a second registration is now being sought to cover this first published edition; or (2) someone other than the author is identified as copyright claimant in the earlier registration, and the author is now seeking registration in his or her own name. If either of these two exceptions applies, check the appropriate box and give the earlier registration number and date. Otherwise, do not submit Form PA; instead, write the Copyright

Office for information about supplementary registration or recordation of transfers of copyright ownership.

Changed Version: If the work has been changed and you are now seeking registration to cover the additions or revisions, check the last box in space 5, give the earlier registration number and date, and complete both parts of space 6 in accordance with the instructions below.

Previous Registration Number and Date: If more than one previous registration has been made for the work, give the number and date of the latest registration.

6 SPACE 6: Derivative Work or Compilation

General Instructions: Complete space 6 if this work is a "changed version," "compilation," or "derivative work," and if it incorporates one or more earlier works that have already been published or registered for copyright or that have fallen into the public domain. A "compilation" is defined as "a work formed by the collection and assembling of preexisting materials or of data that are selected, coordinated, or arranged in such a way that the resulting work as a whole constitutes an original work of authorship." A "derivative work" is "a work based on one or more preexisting works." Examples of derivative works include musical arrangements, dramatizations, translations, condensations, abridgments, motion picture versions, or "any other form in which a work may be recast, transformed, or adapted." Derivative works also include works "consisting of editorial revisions, annotations, or other modifications" if these changes, as a whole, represent an original work of authorship.

Preexisting Material (space 6a): Complete this space **and** space 6b for derivative works. In this space identify the preexisting work that has been recast, transformed, or adapted. For example, the preexisting material might be: "French version of Hugo's 'Le Roi s'amuse'." Do not complete this space for compilations.

Material Added to This Work (space 6b): Give a brief, general statement of the **additional** new material covered by the copyright claim for which registration is sought. In the case of a derivative work, identify this new material. Examples: "Arrangement for piano and orchestra"; "Dramatization for television"; "New film version"; "Revisions throughout; Act III completely new." If the work is a compilation, give a brief, general statement describing both the material that has been compiled **and** the compilation itself. Example: "Compilation of 19th Century Military Songs."

7,8,9 SPACE 7, 8, 9: Fee, Correspondence, Certification, Return Address

Deposit Account: If you maintain a Deposit Account in the Copyright Office, identify it in space 7a. Otherwise, leave the space blank and send the fee of $30 with your application and deposit.

Correspondence (space 7b): This space should contain the name, address, area code, telephone number, fax number, and email address (if available) of the person to be consulted if correspondence about this application becomes necessary.

Certification (space 8): The application cannot be accepted unless it bears the date and the **handwritten signature** of the author or other copyright claimant, or of the owner of exclusive rights, or of the duly authorized agent of the author, claimant, or owner of exclusive right(s).

Address for Return of Certificate (space 9): The address box must be completed legibly since the certificate will be returned in a window envelope.

MORE INFORMATION

How to Register a Recorded Work: If the musical or dramatic work that you are registering has been recorded (as a tape, disk, or cassette), you may choose either copyright application Form PA (Performing Arts) or Form SR (Sound Recordings), depending on the purpose of the registration.

Form PA should be used to register the underlying musical composition or dramatic work. Form SR has been developed specifically to register a "sound recording" as defined by the Copyright Act—a work resulting from the "fixation of a series of sounds," separate and distinct from the underlying musical or dramatic work. Form SR should be used when the copyright claim is limited to the sound recording itself. (In one instance, Form SR may also be used to file for a copyright registration for both kinds of works—see (4) below.) Therefore:

(1) File Form PA if you are seeking to register the musical or dramatic work, not the "sound recording," even though what you deposit for copyright purposes may be in the form of a phonorecord.

(2) File Form PA if you are seeking to register the audio portion of an audiovisual work, such as a motion picture soundtrack; these are considered integral parts of the audiovisual work.

(3) File Form SR if you are seeking to register the "sound recording" itself, that is, the work that results from the fixation of a series of musical, spoken, or other sounds, but not the underlying musical or dramatic work.

(4) File Form SR if you are the copyright claimant for both the underlying musical or dramatic work and the sound recording, *and* you prefer to register both on the same form.

(5) File both forms PA and SR if the copyright claimant for the underlying work and sound recording differ, or you prefer to have separate registration for them.

"Copies" and "Phonorecords": To register for copyright, you are required to deposit "copies" or "phonorecords." These are defined as follows:

Musical compositions may be embodied (fixed) in "copies," objects from which a work can be read or visually perceived, directly or with the aid of a machine or device, such as manuscripts, books, sheet music, film, and videotape. They may also be fixed in "phonorecords," objects embodying fixations of sounds, such as tapes and phonograph disks, commonly known as phonograph records. For example, a song (the work to be registered) can be reproduced in sheet music ("copies") or phonograph records ("phonorecords"), or both.

Copyright Office fees are subject to change.
For current fees, check the Copyright Office
website at *www.copyright.gov*, write the Copyright Office, or call (202) 707-3000.

Ⓒ Form PA
For a Work of Performing Arts
UNITED STATES COPYRIGHT OFFICE

REGISTRATION NUMBER

_____

PA _____ PAU _____
EFFECTIVE DATE OF REGISTRATION

_____
Month   Day   Year

DO NOT WRITE ABOVE THIS LINE. IF YOU NEED MORE SPACE, USE A SEPARATE CONTINUATION SHEET.

1

TITLE OF THIS WORK ▼

PREVIOUS OR ALTERNATIVE TITLES ▼

NATURE OF THIS WORK ▼ See instructions

2

a

NAME OF AUTHOR ▼

DATES OF BIRTH AND DEATH
Year Born ▼   Year Died ▼

Was this contribution to the work a "work made for hire"?
☐ Yes
☐ No

AUTHOR'S NATIONALITY OR DOMICILE
Name of Country
OR { Citizen of _____
Domiciled in _____

WAS THIS AUTHOR'S CONTRIBUTION TO THE WORK
Anonymous?   ☐ Yes ☐ No
Pseudonymous? ☐ Yes ☐ No
If the answer to either of these questions is "Yes," see detailed instructions.

NATURE OF AUTHORSHIP Briefly describe nature of material created by this author in which copyright is claimed. ▼

NOTE

Under the law, the "author" of a "work made for hire" is generally the employer, not the employee (see instructions). For any part of this work that was "made for hire" check "Yes" in the space provided, give the employer (or other person for whom the work was prepared) as "Author" of that part, and leave the space for dates of birth and death blank.

b

NAME OF AUTHOR ▼

DATES OF BIRTH AND DEATH
Year Born ▼   Year Died ▼

Was this contribution to the work a "work made for hire"?
☐ Yes
☐ No

AUTHOR'S NATIONALITY OR DOMICILE
Name of Country
OR { Citizen of _____
Domiciled in _____

WAS THIS AUTHOR'S CONTRIBUTION TO THE WORK
Anonymous?   ☐ Yes ☐ No
Pseudonymous? ☐ Yes ☐ No
If the answer to either of these questions is "Yes," see detailed instructions.

NATURE OF AUTHORSHIP Briefly describe nature of material created by this author in which copyright is claimed. ▼

c

NAME OF AUTHOR ▼

DATES OF BIRTH AND DEATH
Year Born ▼   Year Died ▼

Was this contribution to the work a "work made for hire"?
☐ Yes
☐ No

AUTHOR'S NATIONALITY OR DOMICILE
Name of Country
OR { Citizen of _____
Domiciled in _____

WAS THIS AUTHOR'S CONTRIBUTION TO THE WORK
Anonymous?   ☐ Yes ☐ No
Pseudonymous? ☐ Yes ☐ No
If the answer to either of these questions is "Yes," see detailed instructions.

NATURE OF AUTHORSHIP Briefly describe nature of material created by this author in which copyright is claimed. ▼

3

a YEAR IN WHICH CREATION OF THIS WORK WAS COMPLETED This information must be given Year in all cases.

b DATE AND NATION OF FIRST PUBLICATION OF THIS PARTICULAR WORK Complete this information ONLY if this work has been published.
Month _____ Day _____ Year _____
Nation

4

See instructions before completing this space.

COPYRIGHT CLAIMANT(S) Name and address must be given even if the claimant is the same as the author given in space 2. ▼

TRANSFER If the claimant(s) named here in space 4 is (are) different from the author(s) named in space 2, give a brief statement of how the claimant(s) obtained ownership of the copyright. ▼

DO NOT WRITE HERE OFFICE USE ONLY

APPLICATION RECEIVED

ONE DEPOSIT RECEIVED

TWO DEPOSITS RECEIVED

FUNDS RECEIVED

MORE ON BACK ▶ • Complete all applicable spaces (numbers 5-9) on the reverse side of this page.
• See detailed instructions.   • Sign the form at line 8.

DO NOT WRITE HERE
Page 1 of _____ pages

EXAMINED BY		FORM PA
CHECKED BY		
CORRESPONDENCE ☐ Yes		FOR COPYRIGHT OFFICE USE ONLY

DO NOT WRITE ABOVE THIS LINE. IF YOU NEED MORE SPACE, USE A SEPARATE CONTINUATION SHEET.

PREVIOUS REGISTRATION Has registration for this work, or for an earlier version of this work, already been made in the Copyright Office?
☐ Yes ☐ No If your answer is "Yes," why is another registration being sought? (Check appropriate box.) ▼ If your answer is No, do **not** check box A, B, or C.

a. ☐ This is the first published edition of a work previously registered in unpublished form.

b. ☐ This is the first application submitted by this author as copyright claimant.

c. ☐ This is a changed version of the work, as shown by space 6 on this application.

If your answer is "Yes," give: **Previous Registration Number** ▼   **Year of Registration** ▼

5

DERIVATIVE WORK OR COMPILATION Complete both space 6a and 6b for a derivative work; complete only 6b for a compilation.
Preexisting Material Identify any preexisting work or works that this work is based on or incorporates. ▼

a

6

Material Added to This Work Give a brief, general statement of the material that has been added to this work and in which copyright is claimed. ▼

b

See instructions before completing this space.

DEPOSIT ACCOUNT If the registration fee is to be charged to a Deposit Account established in the Copyright Office, give name and number of Account.
Name ▼   **Account Number** ▼

a

7

CORRESPONDENCE Give name and address to which correspondence about this application should be sent. Name / Address / Apt / City / State / ZIP ▼

b

Area code and daytime telephone number   (   )   Fax number   (   )

Email

CERTIFICATION* I, the undersigned, hereby certify that I am the
Check only one ▶
☐ author
☐ other copyright claimant
☐ owner of exclusive right(s)
☐ authorized agent of _____
Name of author or other copyright claimant, or owner of exclusive right(s) ▲

of the work identified in this application and that the statements made by me in this application are correct to the best of my knowledge.

8

Typed or printed name and date ▼ If this application gives a date of publication in space 3, do not sign and submit it before that date.

Date _____

Handwritten signature (X) ▼

☞   x _____

Certificate will be mailed in window envelope to this address:	Name ▼	
	Number/Street/Apt ▼	
	City/State/ZIP ▼	

YOU MUST:
• Complete all necessary spaces
• Sign your application in space 8
SEND ALL 3 ELEMENTS IN THE SAME PACKAGE:
1. Application form
2. Nonrefundable filing fee in check or money order payable to Register of Copyrights
3. Deposit material
MAIL TO:
Library of Congress
Copyright Office
101 Independence Avenue, S.E.
Washington, D.C. 20559-6000

Fees are subject to change. For current fees, check the Copyright Office website at www.copyright.gov, write the Copyright Office, or call (202) 707-3000.

9

Copyright
United States Copyright Office

Copyright Registration for Sound Recordings

What Is a Sound Recording?

The copyright code of the United States (title 17 of the U.S. Code) provides for copyright protection in sound recordings. Sound recordings are defined in the law as "works that result from the fixation of a series of musical, spoken, or other sounds, but not including the sounds accompanying a motion picture or other audiovisual work." Common examples include recordings of music, drama, or lectures.

Copyright in a sound recording protects the particular series of sounds "fixed" (embodied in a recording) against unauthorized reproduction and revision, unauthorized distribution of phonorecords containing those sounds, and certain unauthorized performances by means of a digital audio transmission. The Digital Performance Right in Sound Recordings Act of 1995, P.L. 104-39, effective February 1, 1996, created a new limited performance right for certain digital transmissions of sound recordings.

Generally, copyright protection extends to two elements in a sound recording: (1) the contribution of the performer(s) whose performance is captured and (2) the contribution of the person or persons responsible for capturing and processing the sounds to make the final recording.

A sound recording is not the same as a *phonorecord*. A phonorecord is the physical object in which works of authorship are embodied. Throughout this circular the word "phonorecord" includes cassette tapes, CDs, LPs, 45 r.p.m. discs, as well as other formats.

NOTE: Sound recordings fixed before February 15, 1972, were generally protected by common law or in some cases by statutes enacted in certain states but were not protected by federal copyright law. In 1971 Congress amended the copyright code to provide copyright protection for sound recordings fixed and first published with the statutory copyright notice on or after February 15, 1972. The 1976 Copyright Act, effective January 1, 1978, provides federal copyright protection for unpublished and published sound recordings fixed on or after February 15, 1972. Any rights or remedies under state law for sound recordings fixed before February 15, 1972, are not annulled or limited by the 1976 Copyright Act until February 15, 2047.

Under the Uruguay Round Agreements Act, effective January 1, 1996, copyright was restored for certain unpublished foreign sound recordings fixed before February 15, 1972, and for certain foreign sound recordings originally published without notice. For further information, request Circular 38B, *Highlights of Copyright Amendments Contained in the Uruguay Round Agreements Act (URAA)*.

© 56.0104

Copyright Registration for Sound Recordings

General Information

Copyright Protection Is Automatic

Under the 1976 Copyright Act, which became effective January 1, 1978, a work is automatically protected by copyright when it is created. A work is created when it is "fixed" in a copy or phonorecord for the first time. Neither registration in the Copyright Office nor publication is required for copyright protection under the present law.

Advantages to Copyright Registration

There are, however, certain advantages to registration, including the establishment of a public record of the copyright claim. Except for certain foreign works, copyright registration must generally be made before an infringement suit may be brought. Timely registration may also provide a broader range of remedies for an infringement of copyright.

Publication

Publication as defined by the 1976 Copyright Act is the distribution of copies or phonorecords of a work to the public by sale or other transfer of ownership or by rental, lease, or lending. The offering to distribute copies or phonorecords to a group of persons for purposes of further distribution, public performance, or public display constitutes publication. A public performance or display of a work does not of itself constitute publication.

"To the public" generally means to persons under no explicit or implicit restrictions with respect to disclosure. The following acts do *not* constitute publication: performing the work, preparing copies or phonorecords, or sending the work to the Copyright Office.

The above definition of publication applies *only* to works governed by the 1976 copyright Act, which took effect January 1, 1978. For information about works published prior to 1978, call the Copyright Office at (202) 707-3000. Recorded information is available 24 hours a day, 7 days a week. Information specialists are on duty from 8:30 a.m. to 5 p.m., eastern time, Monday through Friday, except federal holidays. The TTY number is (202) 707-6737.

Registration Procedures

If you choose to register a claim in your work, send the following three elements together in the same envelope:

1   A properly completed application form;

2   A nonreturnable deposit of the work to be registered; and

3   A nonrefundable filing fee of $30* in the form of a check or money order payable to *Register of Copyrights* with each application. Send the items to:

Library of Congress
Copyright Office
101 Independence Avenue, S.E.
Washington, D.C. 20559-6000

*NOTE: Copyright Office fees are subject to change. For current fees, please check the Copyright Office website at *www.copyright.gov*, write the Copyright Office, or call (202) 707-3000.

Choosing the Appropriate Form

Copyright registration for a sound recording alone is neither the same as, nor a substitute for, registration for the musical, dramatic, or literary work recorded. The underlying work may be registered in its own right apart from any recording of the performance, or in certain cases, the underlying work may be registered together with the sound recording.

When to Use Form SR

Use Form SR for registration of published or unpublished sound recordings, that is, for registration of the particular sounds or recorded performance.

Form SR must also be used if you wish to make one registration for *both* the sound recording *and* the underlying work (the musical composition, dramatic, or literary work). You may make a single registration *only* if the copyright claimant is the same for both the sound recording and the underlying work. In this case, the authorship statement in Space 2 should specify that the claim covers both works.

Form SR is also the appropriate form for registration of a multimedia kit that combines two or more kinds of authorship including a sound recording (such as a kit containing a book and an audiocassette).

When to Use Form PA

For registration purposes, musical compositions and dramatic works that are recorded on discs or cassettes are works of the performing arts and should be registered on Form PA or Short Form PA. Therefore, if you wish to register only the underlying work that is a musical composition or dramatic work, use Form PA even though you may send a disc or cassette for your deposit. For information on Short Form PA, see SL-7, *Short Forms Available*.

NOTE: *Sounds accompanying a motion picture or other audio-visual work* should *not* be registered on Form SR. The copyright law does not define these sounds as "sound recordings" but as an integral part of the motion picture or audiovisual work in which they are incorporated. These sounds are classified as works of the performing arts and should be registered on Form PA.

Examples of the Proper Use of Forms PA and SR

Jane Smith composes words and music, which she entitles "Blowing in the Breeze." Even though she records it, she is not interested in registering the particular recording but only in registering the composition itself. If she decides to submit "Blowing in the Breeze" for copyright registration, she should use Form PA.

Emily Tree performs and records Jane Smith's "Blowing in the Breeze" after complying with permissions and license procedures. If Emily decides to submit her recording for copyright registration, she should use Form SR.

The same principles apply to literary and dramatic works. A recorded performance of an actor speaking lines from "Hamlet" could be registered on Form SR as a sound recording. The claimant in the sound recording, of course, has no copyright in the underlying work, "Hamlet."

How to Complete Form SR

Instructions for completing each space of the application accompany the form. Nevertheless, registration is often delayed because of mistakes or omissions in filling out the form. The following points should be helpful.

Space 1: Title. Give the title of the work exactly as it appears on the phonorecord.

Two or more *unpublished* works registered as a collection must be given a single *collection title*. The individual titles may be given in Space 1 following the collection title or on a Continuation Sheet. For more information on unpublished collections, see page 5 in this circular or request Circular 50, *Copyright Registration for Musical Compositions*.

Space 2: Name of Author. The author of a sound recording is the performer(s) or record producer or both. If the work is "made for hire" as defined below, the *employer* is considered to be the author and should be named in Space 2.

A "work made for hire" is:

1 a work prepared by an employee within the scope of his or her employment, *or*

2 a work of a type specified in the law which has been specially ordered or commissioned, where there is an express written agreement signed by both parties that the work shall be considered a "work made for hire."

Generally speaking, for a new sound recording to be a work made for hire, it must be made by an employee within his or her scope of employment. For more information on works made for hire, see Circular 9, *Works Made for Hire Under the 1976 Copyright Act*.

NOTE: A sound recording is *not* one of the types of works affected by clause (2) of the definition of "work made for hire" unless it constitutes a supplementary work, collective work, or compilation.

Check "yes" to the "work made for hire" question *only* if the conditions for "work made for hire" have been met, and name the employer as the author in Space 2.

Nature of Authorship: *Do not leave this space blank; it must be completed.* Sound recording authorship is the performance, sound production, or both, that is fixed in the recording deposited for registration. Describe this authorship in Space 2 as "sound recording." Space 2 of Form SR must specifically refer to the sound recording authorship in order for this authorship to be included in the registration.

If the claim also covers the underlying work(s), include the appropriate authorship terms for each author, for example, "words," "music," "arrangement of music," or "text." For the claim to cover both the sound recording and the underlying work(s), every author should have contributed to both the sound recording *and* the underlying work(s).

If the claim includes artwork or photographs, include the appropriate term in the statement of authorship.

Space 3: Creation. The year of creation of a sound recording is the year in which the sounds are fixed in a phonorecord for the first time. If the claim extends only to the compilation of preexisting sound recordings, give the year in which the *compilation* was fixed. *The year of creation must always be given.*

Publication: If publication has not taken place, *leave this part of Space 3 blank.* If the work for which registration is sought has been published, give the month, day, and year and nation where the phonorecords were first published.

Space 4: Copyright Claimant(s). The *name* and *address* of the *copyright claimant(s) must be given.* The copyright claimant is either the author or a person or organization to whom the author has transferred *all* of the rights in the United States copyright. When the claimant named is *not* the author,

Copyright Registration for Sound Recordings

a brief *transfer* statement is required at Space 4 to show how the claimant acquired the copyright. Examples of generally acceptable statements include: "by written agreement"; "assignment"; "written contract"; and "by will." Do not attach copies of documents of copyright transfer to the application. For information on how to record transfers or other documents pertaining to a copyright, see Circular 12, *Recordation of Transfers and Other Documents.*

When the name of the claimant is not the name of the author given at Space 2 but the two names identify one person, the relationship between the names should be explained at Space 4. Examples are: "Doe Recording Company, solely owned by John Doe" or "John Doe doing business as Doe Recording Company."

Space 5: Previous Registrations. If no *previous registration* has been made, answer the first question "no" and leave the rest of Space 5 blank.

The first question should be answered "yes" *only* if a previous registration for this work or another version of it was completed and a certificate of copyright registration issued.

If this is the case, check the appropriate box to show why another registration is sought *and* give the requested information about the previous registration.

Space 6: Derivative Works. A derivative sound recording is one which incorporates some preexisting sounds — sounds which were previously registered, previously published, or which were fixed before February 15, 1972. Registration for a derivative work must be based on the new authorship that has been added. When a work contains preexisting sounds, Space 6 of the application must contain brief, general descriptions of both the preexisting material (Space 6a) and the added material (Space 6b).

For example, Fine Sounds Corporation issues a CD-album containing 10 selections, 2 of which were published last month as singles. On the application for registration of the sounds on the album, the following statement might be given in Space 6a: "sounds for tracks 1 and 3, previously published." The new material might be described in Space 6b as "sounds for 8 tracks" or "sounds for 8 selections."

Appropriate Form for Copyright Registration of Domestic Works

The work being registered	Form	How to describe the authorship in Space 2 "Nature of Authorship"	What should be deposited *Published in the United States*	What should be deposited *Unpublished*
Author creates a song, recorded by independent group; can claim copyright in the song	PA	Music and Words *or* Music	1 phonorecord (disc, if published in disc form)	1 complete phonorecord (usually disc or cassette)
Vocalist and band perform and record musical work; can claim copyright in the recorded performance only	SR	Sound Recording	2 complete phonorecords (discs, if published in disc form)	1 complete phonorecord
Author creates music and performs it, recording the performance; can claim copyright both in the music and the recording	SR	Music and Sound Recording *or* Music, Words, and Sound Recording	2 complete phonorecords (discs, if published in disc form)	1 complete phonorecord
Author writes a play and records it, but can claim copyright only in the play itself, not in recorded performance	PA	Script	1 complete phonorecord (disc, if published in disc form)	1 complete phonorecord
Author writes poem or narrative and records it, can claim copyright both in text and in recorded performance	SR	Text and Sound Recording	2 complete phonorecords (discs, if published in disc form)	1 complete phonorecord
Author creates musical composition in machine-readable copy (*e.g.*, computer floppy disk) and can claim copyright in only musical composition	PA	Music *or* Music and Words	Transcription of entire work in score or on audio cassette	Transcription of entire work in score or on audio cassette
Author creates musical composition in machine-readable copy (*e.g.*, computer floppy disk) and can claim copyright in both composition and performance	SR	Music and Sound Recording *or* Music, Words, and Sound Recording	Reproduction of entire work on audio cassette	Reproduction of entire work on audio cassette
Author creates musical composition on CD-ROM and can claim copyright in both music and sound recording	SR	Music and Sound Recording	1 complete CD-ROM package	1 complete CD-ROM package

Points to note: *Do not leave Space 2 blank. Do not use "entire work" to describe "nature of authorship." Deposit the "best edition" of a published work.*

In cases where the preexisting sounds themselves have been altered or changed in character, Space 6b should be used to describe in more precise terms the engineering techniques involved. For example, Educational Records, Inc., remixes the original tracks of a previously released recording of a Beethoven symphony. Space 6a should identify the preexisting material as "sounds previously published." Space 6b might indicate "remixed from multitrack sound sources" or "remixed sounds." This new material must result from creative new authorship rather than mere mechanical processes; if only a few slight variations or purely mechanical changes (such as declicking or remastering) have been made, registration is not possible.

Compilation of Sound Recordings: A "compilation" is a work formed by the collecting and assembling of preexisting materials that are selected, coordinated, or arranged in such a way that the resulting work as a whole constitutes an original work of authorship.

When an author contributes a certain minimum amount of authorship in the selection and ordering of *preexisting* sound recordings, the author produces a copyrightable compilation. The copyright in the compilation of recordings is separate and distinct from copyright (if any) in the recordings themselves. It extends *only* to the selection and ordering of the recordings on the disc or tape.

Fill out part b of Space 6. Describe the new material as "compilation of sound recordings." In Space 2, use the same statement to describe the nature of the author's contribution. *For example*: Oldies Record Company has chosen the greatest hits of the big bands recorded in the thirties and forties and published them in a boxed set of discs. The authorship involved in choosing the bands, selecting their "greatest hits," selecting the particular recordings, and ordering them on the discs may be registered as a compilation, even though the recordings themselves are not protected by the federal copyright code because they were fixed prior to February 15, 1972.

Space 8: Certifications. The application must bear an *original signature* and be *dated*. Stamped signatures are not acceptable. For a published work, the application must be certified on or after the date of publication. Please type or print neatly using black ink. The form is used to produce the certificate.

Registration of Unpublished Collections

For registration purposes, a sound recording is a single work. It may be possible to include a claim in the sound recording along with a claim in a group of unpublished recorded musical works as a single collection, provided the conditions discussed below are met.

As a general rule, a number of unpublished musical works may be grouped together and registered as a single collection with one application *only if the author(s) and the copyright owner(s) are the same for every work*. For the registration to cover the sound recording as well, this same condition must apply to both the musical works and the sound recording.

For example: Al and Sue co-wrote eight songs and performed and recorded them on tape. Because they co-authored all of the songs and the sound recording, they may register all of these elements on one application using Form SR. Space 2 should name both individuals as authors and describe the authorship of each as "lyrics, music, and sound recording." Space 4 should name both of them as claimants.

The application should identify the collection by giving a single collection title in Space 1. The individual titles may be given in the space provided for alternative titles. Although the individual selections are covered by the registration, only the collection title is indexed in the catalog of copyright registrations. Individual titles will appear in the Copyright Office records only if each work is registered separately or if an application for supplementary registration is submitted to specify the individual titles in a collection. An application for supplementary registration may not be submitted until a certificate of registration has been issued for the collection. For more information on supplementary registration, see Circular 8, *Supplementary Copyright Registration*, and application Form CA.

If the authorship and ownership are not the same for each of the musical works, the works must either be registered individually or grouped into two or more collections, each of which meets the unpublished collection requirements. If the requirements have been met for the musical works but not for the sound recording, the sound recording must be registered separately, though both registrations can be filed together using the same disc or tape as the deposit. For further information, request Circular 50, *Copyright Registration for Musical Compositions*.

Deposit Requirements

To register a copyright claim in a sound recording, the deposit requirement is either one or two phonorecords. The number and format required depend upon several factors.

- If unpublished, deposit one phonorecord (tape or disc). Be sure to label it with the title(s). If it is a collection, give the collection title on the label.

Copyright Registration for Sound Recordings

- If first published in the United States *on or after January 1, 1978,* deposit two complete phonorecords of the best edition together with any material, such as record sleeves and jackets, published with the phonorecords.
- If first published in the United States *before January 1, 1978,* deposit two complete phonorecords of the work as first published.
- If first published outside the United States *before March 1, 1989,* deposit one complete phonorecord of the work as first published.
- If first published outside the United States *after March 1, 1989,* deposit one complete phonorecord of either the first published edition or the best edition of the work.

Deposits cannot be returned.

"Best Edition" Requirements

If the sound recording has been published in only one edition, send two phonorecords of that edition.

If it has been published in more than one edition, the "best edition" in descending order of suitability is: (1) a compact digital disc rather than a vinyl disc; (2) a vinyl disc rather than a tape; (3) an open-reel tape rather than a cartridge; and (4) a cartridge rather than a cassette.

Notice of Copyright for Sound Recordings

Before March 1, 1989, the use of copyright notice was mandatory on all published works, and any work first published before that date should have carried a notice. For works first published on and after March 1, 1989, use of the copyright notice is optional. For more information about copyright notice, see Circular 3, *Copyright Notice.*

Mandatory Deposit for Works Published in the United States

Although a copyright registration is not required, the 1976 Copyright Act establishes a mandatory deposit requirement for works published in the United States. In general, the owner of copyright or the owner of the exclusive right of publication in the work has a legal obligation to deposit in the Copyright Office within 3 months of publication in the United States *two* complete phonorecords of the best edition. It is the responsibility of the owner of copyright or the owner of the right of first publication in the work to fulfill this mandatory deposit requirement. Failure to make the deposit

can result in fines and other penalties but does not affect copyright protection.

A "complete phonorecord" in the case of a sound recording includes a phonorecord together with any material published with such phonorecord such as textual or pictorial matter appearing on the album cover or embodied in inserts in the container.

Certain categories of works are entirely exempt from the mandatory deposit requirements, and the obligation is reduced for certain other categories. For further information, see Circular 7D, *Mandatory Deposit of Copies or Phonorecords for the Library of Congress.*

Use of Mandatory Deposit to Satisfy Registration Requirements

The 1976 copyright Act establishes the conditions under which the same deposit of phonorecords will satisfy the deposit requirements for the Library of Congress and for copyright registration. The phonorecords should be sent to the Copyright Office *accompanied* by an *application* for copyright registration and a $30* fee all together in the same mailing package.

The mandatory deposit requirement also applies to sound recordings first published abroad that are later published in this country by the distribution of phonorecords that either are imported or are issued as an American edition. Once the sound recording is registered, the mandatory deposit requirement has been satisfied.

*NOTE: Copyright Office fees are subject to change. For current fees, please check the Copyright Office website at *www.copyright.gov,* write the Copyright Office, or call (202) 707-3000.

Effective Date of Registration

A copyright registration is effective on the date the Copyright Office receives all the required elements in acceptable form, regardless of how long it then takes to process the application and mail the certificate of registration. The time the Copyright Office requires to process an application varies, depending on the amount of material the Office is receiving.

If you apply for copyright registration, you will not receive an acknowledgment that your application has been received (the Office receives more than 600,000 applications annually), but you can expect:

- a letter or a telephone call from a Copyright Office staff member if further information is needed or

- a certificate of registration indicating that the work has been registered, or if the application cannot be accepted, a letter explaining why it has been rejected.

Requests to have certificates available for pickup in the Public Information Office or to have certificates sent by Federal Express or another mail service cannot be honored.

If you want to know the date that the Copyright Office receives your material, send it by registered or certified mail and request a return receipt.

For Further Information

Information via the Internet

Frequently requested circulars, announcements, regulations, other related materials, and all copyright application forms are available via the Internet. You may access these from the Copyright Office website at *www.copyright.gov*.

Information by fax

Circulars and other information (but not application forms) are available by using a touchtone phone to access Fax-on-Demand at (202) 707-2600.

Information by telephone

For general information about copyright, call the Copyright Public Information Office at (202) 707-3000. The TTY number is (202) 707-6737. Information specialists are on duty from 8:30 a.m. to 5:00 p.m., eastern time, Monday through Friday, except federal holidays. Recorded informa-

tion is available 24 hours a day. Or, if you know which application forms and circulars you want, request them 24 hours a day from the Forms and Publications Hotline at (202) 707-9100. Leave a recorded message.

Information by regular mail

Write to:

Library of Congress
Copyright Office
Publications Section, LM-455
101 Independence Avenue, S.E.
Washington, D.C. 20559-6000

For a list of other material published by the Copyright Office, request Circular 2, *Publications on Copyright*.

The Copyright Public Information Office is open to the public 8:30 a.m. to 5:00 p.m., Monday through Friday, eastern time, except federal holidays. The office is located in the Library of Congress, James Madison Memorial Building, Room 401, at 101 Independence Avenue, S.E., Washington, D.C., near the Capitol South Metro stop. Information specialists are available to answer questions, provide circulars, and accept applications for registration. Access for disabled individuals is at the front door on Independence Avenue, S.E.

The Copyright Office is not permitted to give legal advice. If information or guidance is needed on matters such as disputes over the ownership of a copyright, suits against possible infringers, the procedure for getting a work published, or the method of obtaining royalty payments, it may be necessary to consult an attorney.

Form SR

Detach and read these instructions before completing this form.
Make sure all applicable spaces have been filled in before you return this form.

BASIC INFORMATION

When to Use This Form: Use Form SR for registration of published or unpublished sound recordings. It should be used when the copyright claim is limited to the sound recording itself. and it may also be used where the same copyright claimant is seeking simultaneous registration of the underlying musical, dramatic, or literary work embodied in the phonorecord.

With one exception, "sound recordings" are works that result from the fixation of a series of musical, spoken, or other sounds. The exception is for the audio portions of audiovisual works, such as a motion picture soundtrack or an audio cassette accompanying a filmstrip. These are considered a part of the audiovisual work as a whole.

Deposit to Accompany Application: An application for copyright registration must be accompanied by a deposit consisting of phonorecords representing the entire work for which registration is to be made.

Unpublished Work: Deposit one complete phonorecord.

Published Work: Deposit two complete phonorecords of the best edition, together with "any printed or other visually perceptible material" published with the phonorecords.

Work First Published Outside the United States: Deposit one complete phonorecord of the first foreign edition.

Contribution to a Collective Work: Deposit one complete phonorecord of the best edition of the collective work.

The Copyright Notice: Before March 1, 1989, the use of copyright notice was mandatory on all published works, and any work first published before that date should have carried a notice. For works first published on and after March 1, 1989, use of the copyright notice is optional. For more information about copyright notice, see Circular 3, "Copyright Notices."

For Further Information: To speak to an information specialist, call (202) 707-3000 (TTY: (202) 707-6737). Recorded information is available 24 hours a day. Order forms and other publications from Library of Congress, Copyright Office, 101 Independence Avenue, S.E., Washington, D.C. 20559-6000 or call the Forms and Publications Hotline at (202) 707-9100. Most circulars (but not forms) are available via fax. Call (202) 707-2600 from a touchtone phone. Access and download circulars, forms, and other information from the Copyright Office Website at *www.copyright.gov.*

PRIVACY ACT ADVISORY STATEMENT Required by the Privacy Act of 1974 (P.L. 93-579)
The authority for requesting this information is title 17, U.S.C., secs. 409 and 410. Furnishing the requested information is voluntary. But if the information is not furnished, it may be necessary to delay or refuse registration and you may not be entitled to certain relief, remedies, and benefits provided in chapters 4 and 5 of title 17, U.S.C.

The principal uses of the requested information are the establishment and maintenance of a public record and the examination of the application for compliance with the registration requirements of the copyright code.

Other routine uses include public inspection and copying, preparation of public indexes, preparation of public catalogs of copyright registrations, and preparation of search reports upon request.

NOTE: No other advisory statement will be given in connection with this application. Please keep this statement and refer to it if we communicate with you regarding this application.

LINE-BY-LINE INSTRUCTIONS

Please type or print neatly using black ink. The form is used to produce the certificate.

1   SPACE 1: Title

Title of This Work: Every work submitted for copyright registration must be given a title to identify that particular work. If the phonorecords or any accompanying printed material bears a title (or an identifying phrase that could serve as a title), transcribe that wording completely and exactly on the application. Indexing of the registration and future identification of the work may depend on the information you give here.

Previous, Alternative, or Contents Titles: Complete this space if there are any previous or alternative titles for the work under which someone searching for the registration might be likely to look, or under which a document pertaining to the work might be recorded. You may also give the individual contents titles, if any, in this space or you may use a Continuation Sheet. Circle the term that describes the titles given.

2   SPACE 2: Author(s)

General Instructions: After reading these instructions, decide who are the "authors" of this work for copyright purposes. Then, unless the work is a "collective work," give the requested information about every "author" who contributed any appreciable amount of copyrightable matter to this version of the work. If you need further space, request additional Continuation Sheets. In the case of a collective work such as a collection of previously published or registered sound recordings, give information about the author of the collective work as a whole. If you are submitting this Form SR to cover the recorded musical, dramatic, or literary work as well as the sound recording itself, it is important for space 2 to include full information about the various authors of all of the material covered by the copyright claim, making clear the nature of each author's contribution.

Name of Author: The fullest form of the author's name should be given. Unless the work was "made for hire," the individual who actually created the work is its "author." In the case of a work made for hire, the statute provides that "the employer or other person for whom the work was prepared is considered the author."

What is a "Work Made for Hire"? A "work made for hire" is defined as: (1) "a work prepared by an employee within the scope of his or her employment;" or (2)

"a work specially ordered or commissioned for use as a contribution to a collective work, as a part of a motion picture or other audiovisual work, as a translation, as a supplementary work, as a compilation, as an instructional text, as answer material for a test, or as an atlas, if the parties expressly agree in a written instrument signed by them that the work shall be considered a work made for hire." If you have checked "Yes" to indicate that the work was "made for hire," you must give the full legal name of the employer (or other person for whom the work was prepared). You may also include the name of the employee along with the name of the employer (for example: "Elster Record Co., employer for hire of John Ferguson").

"Anonymous" or "Pseudonymous" Work: An author's contribution to a work is "anonymous" if that author is not identified on the copies or phonorecords of the work. An author's contribution to a work is "pseudonymous" if that author is identified on the copies or phonorecords under a fictitious name. If the work is "anonymous" you may: (1) leave the line blank; or (2) state "anonymous" on the line; or (3) reveal the author's identity. If the work is "pseudonymous" you may: (1) leave the line blank; or (2) give the pseudonym and identify it as such (for example: "Huntley Haverstock, pseudonym"); or (3) reveal the author's name, making clear which is the real name and which is the pseudonym (for example: "Judith Barton, whose pseudonym is Madeline Elster"). However, the citizenship or domicile of the author **must** be given in all cases.

Dates of Birth and Death: If the author is dead, the statute requires that the year of death be included in the application unless the work is anonymous or pseudonymous. The author's birth date is optional, but is useful as a form of identification. Leave this space blank if the author's contribution was a "work made for hire."

Author's Nationality or Domicile: Give the country in which the author is a citizen, or the country in which the author is domiciled. Nationality or domicile **must** be given in all cases.

Nature of Authorship: Sound recording authorship is the performance, sound production, or both, that is fixed in the recording deposited for registration. Describe this authorship in space 2 as "sound recording." If the claim also covers the underlying work(s), include the appropriate authorship terms for each author, for example, "words," "music," "arrangement of music," or "text."

Generally, for the claim to cover both the sound recording and the underlying work(s), every author should have contributed to both the sound recording **and** the underlying work(s). If the claim includes artwork or photographs, include the appropriate term in the statement of authorship.

3 SPACE 3: Creation and Publication

General Instructions: Do not confuse "creation" with "publication." Every application for copyright registration must state "the year in which creation of the work was completed." Give the date and nation of first publication only if the work has been published.

Creation: Under the statute, a work is "created" when it is fixed in a copy or phonorecord for the first time. Where a work has been prepared over a period of time, the part of the work existing in fixed form on a particular date constitutes the created work on that date. The date you give here should be the year in which the author completed the particular version for which registration is now being sought, even if other versions exist or if further changes or additions are planned.

Publication: The statute defines "publication" as "the distribution of copies or phonorecords of a work to the public by sale or other transfer of ownership, or by rental, lease, or lending"; a work is also "published" if there has been an "offering to distribute copies or phonorecords to a group of persons for purposes of further distribution, public performance, or public display." Give the full date (month, date, year) when, and the country where, publication first occurred. If first publication took place simultaneously in the United States and other countries, it is sufficient to state "U.S.A."

4 SPACE 4: Claimant(s)

Name(s) and Address(es) of Copyright Claimant(s): Give the name(s) and address(es) of the copyright claimant(s) in the work even if the claimant is the same as the author. Copyright in a work belongs initially to the author of the work (including, in the case of a work made for hire, the employer or other person for whom the work was prepared). The copyright claimant is either the author of the work or a person or organization to whom the copyright initially belonging to the author has been transferred.

Transfer: The statute provides that, if the copyright claimant is not the author, the application for registration must contain "a brief statement of how the claimant obtained ownership of the copyright." If any copyright claimant named in space 4a is not an author named in space 2, give a brief statement explaining how the claimant(s) obtained ownership of the copyright. Examples: "By written contract"; "Transfer of all rights by author"; "Assignment"; "By will." Do not attach transfer documents or other attachments or riders.

5 SPACE 5: Previous Registration

General Instructions: The questions in space 5 are intended to show whether an earlier registration has been made for this work and, if so, whether there is any basis for a new registration. As a rule, only one basic copyright registration can be made for the same version of a particular work.

Same Version: If this version is substantially the same as the work covered by a previous registration, a second registration is not generally possible unless: (1) the work has been registered in unpublished form and a second registration is now being sought to cover this first published edition; or (2) someone other than the author is identified as copyright claimant in the earlier registration and the author is now seeking registration in his or her own name. If either of these two exceptions applies, check the appropriate box and give the earlier registration number and date. Otherwise, do not submit Form SR. Instead, write the Copyright Office for information about supplementary registration or recordation of transfers of copyright ownership.

Changed Version: If the work has been changed and you are now seeking registration to cover the additions or revisions, check the last box in space 5, give the earlier registration number and date, and complete both parts of space 6 in accordance with the instructions below.

Previous Registration Number and Date: If more than one previous registration has been made for the work, give the number and date of the latest registration.

6 SPACE 6: Derivative Work or Compilation

General Instructions: Complete space 6 if this work is a "changed version," "compilation," or "derivative work," and if it incorporates one or more earlier works that have already been published or registered for copyright, or that have fallen into the public domain, or sound recordings that were fixed before February 15, 1972. A "compilation" is defined as "a work formed by the collection and assembling of preexisting materials or of data that are selected, coordinated, or arranged in such a way that the resulting work as a whole constitutes an original work of authorship." A "derivative work" is "a work based on one or more preexisting works." Examples of derivative works include recordings reissued with substantial editorial revisions or abridgments of the recorded sounds, and recordings republished with new recorded material, or "any other form in which a work may be recast, transformed, or adapted." Derivative works also include works "consisting of editorial revisions, annotations, or other modifications" if these changes, as a whole, represent an original work of authorship.

Preexisting Material (space 6a): Complete this space and space 6b for derivative works. In this space identify the preexisting work that has been recast, transformed, or adapted. The preexisting work may be material that has been previously published, previously registered, or that is in the public domain. For example, the preexisting material might be: "1970 recording by Sperryville Symphony of Bach Double Concerto."

Material Added to This Work (space 6b): Give a brief, general statement of the additional new material covered by the copyright claim for which registration is sought. In the case of a derivative work, identify this new material. Examples: "Recorded performances on bands 1 and 3"; "Remixed sounds from original multitrack sound sources"; "New words, arrangement, and additional sounds." If the work is a compilation, give a brief, general statement describing both the material that has been compiled and the compilation itself. Example: "Compilation of 1938 Recordings by various swing bands."

7, 8, 9 SPACE 7,8,9: Fee, Correspondence, Certification, Return Address

Deposit Account: If you maintain a Deposit Account in the Copyright Office, identify it in space 7a. Otherwise, leave the space blank and send the filing fee of $30 with your application and deposit. (See space 8 on form.) (Note: Copyright Office fees are subject to change. For current fees, please check the Copyright Office website at www.copyright.gov, write the Copyright Office, or call (202) 707-3000.)

Correspondence (space 7b): This space should contain the name, address, area code, telephone number, fax number, and email address (if available) of the person to be consulted if correspondence about this application becomes necessary.

Certification (space 8): This application cannot be accepted unless it bears the date and the **handwritten signature** of the author or other copyright claimant, or of the owner of exclusive right(s), or of the duly authorized agent of the author, claimant, or owner of exclusive right(s).

Address for Return of Certificate (space 9): The address box must be completed legibly since the certificate will be returned in a window envelope.

MORE INFORMATION

"Works": "Works" are the basic subject matter of copyright; they are what authors create and copyright protects. The statute draws a sharp distinction between the "work" and "any material object in which the work is embodied."

"Copies" and "Phonorecords": These are the two types of material objects in which "works" are embodied. In general, **"copies"** are objects from which a work can be read or visually perceived, directly or with the aid of a machine or device, such as manuscripts, books, sheet music, film, and videotape. **"Phonorecords"** are objects embodying fixations of sounds, such as audio tapes and phonograph disks. For example, a song (the "work") can be reproduced in sheet music ("copies") or phonograph disks ("phonorecords"), or both.

"Sound Recordings": These are "works," not "copies" or "phonorecords." "Sound recordings" are "works that result from the fixation of a series of musical, spoken, or other sounds, but not including the sounds accompanying a motion picture or other audiovisual work." Example: When a record company issues a new release, the release will typically involve two distinct "works": the "musical work" that has been recorded, and the "sound recording" as a separate work in itself. The material objects that the record company sends out are "phonorecords": physical reproductions of both the "musical work" and the "sound recording."

Should You File More Than One Application? If your work consists of a recorded musical, dramatic, or literary work and if both the "work" and the sound recording as a separate "work" are eligible for registration, the application form you should file depends on the following:

File Only Form SR if: The copyright claimant is the same for both the musical, dramatic, or literary work and for the sound recording, and you are seeking a single registration to cover both of these "works."

File Only Form PA (or Form TX) if: You are seeking to register only the musical, dramatic, or literary work, not the sound recording. Form PA is appropriate for works of the performing arts; Form TX is for nondramatic literary works.

Separate Applications Should Be Filed on Form PA (or Form TX) and on Form SR if: (1) The copyright claimant for the musical, dramatic, or literary work is different from the copyright claimant for the sound recording; or (2) You prefer to have separate registrations for the musical, dramatic, or literary work and for the sound recording.

Copyright Office fees are subject to change. For current fees, check the Copyright Office website at *www.copyright.gov*, write the Copyright Office, or call (202) 707-3000.

Form SR
For a Sound Recording
UNITED STATES COPYRIGHT OFFICE

REGISTRATION NUMBER

_____

SR   SRU
EFFECTIVE DATE OF REGISTRATION

Month   Day   Year

DO NOT WRITE ABOVE THIS LINE. IF YOU NEED MORE SPACE, USE A SEPARATE CONTINUATION SHEET.

1

TITLE OF THIS WORK ▼

PREVIOUS, ALTERNATIVE, OR CONTENTS TITLES (CIRCLE ONE) ▼

2   a

NAME OF AUTHOR ▼

DATES OF BIRTH AND DEATH
Year Born ▼   Year Died ▼

Was this contribution to the work a "work made for hire"?
☐ Yes
☐ No

AUTHOR'S NATIONALITY OR DOMICILE
Name of Country
OR { Citizen of ▶ _____
Domiciled in ▶ _____

WAS THIS AUTHOR'S CONTRIBUTION TO THE WORK
Anonymous?   ☐ Yes ☐ No
Pseudonymous?   ☐ Yes ☐ No

If the answer to either of these questions is "Yes," see detailed instructions.

NATURE OF AUTHORSHIP   Briefly describe nature of material created by this author in which copyright is claimed. ▼

NOTE

Under the law, the "author" of a "work made for hire" is generally the employer, not the employee (see instructions). For any part of this work that was "made for hire," check "Yes" in the space provided, give the employer (or other person for whom the work was prepared) as "Author" of that part, and leave the space for dates of birth and death blank.

b   NAME OF AUTHOR ▼

DATES OF BIRTH AND DEATH
Year Born ▼   Year Died ▼

Was this contribution to the work a "work made for hire"?
☐ Yes
☐ No

AUTHOR'S NATIONALITY OR DOMICILE
Name of Country
OR { Citizen of ▶ _____
Domiciled in ▶ _____

WAS THIS AUTHOR'S CONTRIBUTION TO THE WORK
Anonymous?   ☐ Yes ☐ No
Pseudonymous?   ☐ Yes ☐ No

If the answer to either of these questions is "Yes," see detailed instructions.

NATURE OF AUTHORSHIP   Briefly describe nature of material created by this author in which copyright is claimed. ▼

c   NAME OF AUTHOR ▼

DATES OF BIRTH AND DEATH
Year Born ▼   Year Died ▼

Was this contribution to the work a "work made for hire"?
☐ Yes
☐ No

AUTHOR'S NATIONALITY OR DOMICILE
Name of Country
OR { Citizen of ▶ _____
Domiciled in ▶ _____

WAS THIS AUTHOR'S CONTRIBUTION TO THE WORK
Anonymous?   ☐ Yes ☐ No
Pseudonymous?   ☐ Yes ☐ No

If the answer to either of these questions is "Yes," see detailed instructions.

NATURE OF AUTHORSHIP   Briefly describe nature of material created by this author in which copyright is claimed. ▼

3   a

YEAR IN WHICH CREATION OF THIS WORK WAS COMPLETED
This information must be given in all cases.
◀ Year

b   DATE AND NATION OF FIRST PUBLICATION OF THIS PARTICULAR WORK
Complete this information ONLY if this work has been published.
Month ▶ _____ Day ▶ _____ Year ▶ _____
◀ Nation

4   a

See instructions before completing this space.

COPYRIGHT CLAIMANT(S) Name and address must be given even if the claimant is the same as the author given in space 2. ▼

b   TRANSFER If the claimant(s) named here in space 4 is (are) different from the author(s) named in space 2, give a brief statement of how the claimant(s) obtained ownership of the copyright. ▼

DO NOT WRITE HERE
OFFICE USE ONLY

APPLICATION RECEIVED

ONE DEPOSIT RECEIVED

TWO DEPOSITS RECEIVED

FUNDS RECEIVED

MORE ON BACK ▶   • Complete all applicable spaces (numbers 5-9) on the reverse side of this page.
• See detailed instructions.   • Sign the form at line 8.

DO NOT WRITE HERE
Page 1 of _____ pages

EXAMINED BY	FORM SR
CHECKED BY	
CORRESPONDENCE ☐ Yes	FOR COPYRIGHT OFFICE USE ONLY

DO NOT WRITE ABOVE THIS LINE. IF YOU NEED MORE SPACE, USE A SEPARATE CONTINUATION SHEET.

PREVIOUS REGISTRATION Has registration for this work, or for an earlier version of this work, already been made in the Copyright Office?

☐ Yes ☐ No If your answer is "Yes," why is another registration being sought? (Check appropriate box) ▼

a. ☐ This work was previously registered in unpublished form and now has been published for the first time.

b. ☐ This is the first application submitted by this author as copyright claimant.

c. ☐ This is a changed version of the work, as shown by space 6 on this application.

If your answer is "Yes," give: **Previous Registration Number ▼**   **Year of Registration ▼**

5

DERIVATIVE WORK OR COMPILATION

Preexisting Material Identify any preexisting work or works that this work is based on or incorporates. ▼

a

Material Added to This Work Give a brief, general statement of the material that has been added to this work and in which copyright is claimed. ▼

b

6

See instructions
before completing
this space.

DEPOSIT ACCOUNT If the registration fee is to be charged to a Deposit Account established in the Copyright Office, give name and number of Account.

Name ▼   **Account Number ▼**

a

CORRESPONDENCE Give name and address to which correspondence about this application should be sent.   Name/Address/Apt/City/State/ZIP ▼

b

Area code and daytime telephone number   Fax number

Email

7

CERTIFICATION* I, the undersigned, hereby certify that I am the

Check only one ▼

☐ author

☐ other copyright claimant

☐ owner of exclusive right(s)

☐ authorized agent of _____
Name of author or other copyright claimant, or owner of exclusive right(s) ▲

of the work identified in this application and that the statements made by me in this application are correct to the best of my knowledge.

Typed or printed name and date ▼ If this application gives a date of publication in space 3, do not sign and submit it before that date.

_____   Date _____

Handwritten signature (x) ▼

X _____

8

Certificate will be mailed in window envelope to this address	Name ▼
	Number/Street/Apt ▼
	City/State/ZIP ▼

YOU MUST:
• Complete all necessary spaces
• Sign your application in space 8

SEND ALL 3 ELEMENTS IN THE SAME PACKAGE:
1. Application form
2. Nonrefundable filing fee in check or money order payable to *Register of Copyrights*
3. Deposit material

MAIL TO:
Library of Congress
Copyright Office - SR
101 Independence Avenue, S.E.
Washington, D.C. 20559-6237

Fees are subject to change. For current fees, check the Copyright Office website at www.copyright.gov, write the Copyright Office, or call (202) 707-3000.

9

*17 U.S.C. § 506(e): Any person who knowingly makes a false representation of a material fact in the application for copyright registration provided for by section 409, or in any written statement filed in connection with the application, shall be fined not more than $2,500.

Rev: July 2003—100,000   Web Rev: July 2003   ♻ Printed on recycled paper

U.S. Government Printing Office: 2003-496-605/60,0xx

United States Copyright Office

Circular 56a

Copyright Registration of Musical Compositions and Sound Recordings

This circular explains the difference, for copyright purposes, between **MUSICAL COMPOSITIONS** and **SOUND RECORDINGS**.

A **Musical Composition** consists of music, including any accompanying words, and is normally registered in Class PA. The author of a musical composition is generally the composer, and the lyricist, if any. A musical composition may be in the form of a notated copy (for example, sheet music) **or** in the form of a phonorecord (for example, cassette tape, LP, or CD). Sending a musical composition in the form of a phonorecord does **not** necessarily mean that there is a claim to copyright in the sound recording.

A **Sound Recording** results from the fixation of a series of musical, spoken, or other sounds and is always registered in Class SR. The author of a sound recording is the performer(s) whose performance is fixed, or the record producer who processes the sounds and fixes them in the final recording, or both.

Copyright in a sound recording is not the same as, or a substitute for, copyright in the underlying musical composition.

REGISTRATION OF A MUSICAL COMPOSITION AND A SOUND RECORDING WITH A SINGLE APPLICATION

Although they are separate works, a musical composition and a sound recording may be registered together on a single application if ownership of the copyrights in both is exactly the same. To register a single claim in both works, complete Form SR. Give information about the author(s) of both the musical composition and the sound recording.

USE THIS CHART TO HELP CHOOSE THE APPROPRIATE FORM FOR COPYRIGHT REGISTRATION

POINTS TO NOTE:

· Do not leave Space 2 blank.

· Do not use "entire work" to describe "nature of authorship."

· Deposit the "best edition" of a published work.*

NOTE: Phonorecords (tapes, cassette tapes, cartridges, disks) are not sound recordings.
Phonorecords are physical objects in which various kinds of works can be fixed—the works themselves may be musical compositions, literary works, dramatic works, or sound recordings.

What is being registered:	Form to use:	How to describe "Nature of Authorship" in Space 2:	What should be deposited: Published in the United States*	What should be deposited: Unpublished
1. Song or other musical composition	PA	Music and Words OR Music	2 complete copies (if published in a notated copy) OR 1 phonorecord (if published only on a disk or cassette)	1 complete copy (lead sheet, etc.) OR 1 phonorecord (disk or cassette)
2. Sound Recording only	SR	Sound Recording	2 complete phonorecords	1 complete phonorecord
3. Musical Composition and Sound Recording	SR	Music and Sound Recording OR Music, Words, and Sound Recording	2 complete phonorecords	1 complete phonorecord

NOTE: To make a single registration, copyright ownership in the musical composition and in the sound recording must be the same.

---

* For foreign publications, one copy or phonorecord of either the first published edition or the best edition.

REGISTRATION PROCEDURES

To register your work, send the following material **in the same envelope or package** to:
Library of Congress
Copyright Office
101 Independence Avenue, S.E.
Washington, D.C. 20559-6000:

1. A properly completed application form
2. A nonreturnable, clearly labeled deposit(s) of the work to be registered and
3. A nonrefundable filing fee of $30* for each application

> *** NOTE: Copyright Office fees are subject to change. For current fees, please check the Copyright Office website at *www.copyright.gov*, write the Copyright Office, or call (202) 707-3000.**

EFFECTIVE DATE OF REGISTRATION

A copyright registration is effective on the date the Copyright Office receives all the required elements in acceptable form, regardless of how long it then takes to process the application and mail the certificate of registration. The time the Copyright Office requires to process an application varies, depending on the amount of material the Office is receiving.

If you apply for copyright registration, you will not receive an acknowledgment that your application has been received (the Office receives more than 600,000 applications annually), but you can expect:

- A letter or a telephone call from a Copyright Office staff member if further information is needed or
- A certificate of registration indicating that the work has been registered, or if the application cannot be accepted, a letter explaining why it has been rejected.

Requests to have certificates available for pickup in the Public Information Office or to have certificates sent by Federal Express or another mail service cannot be honored.

If you want to know the date that the Copyright Office receives your material, send it by registered or certified mail and request a return receipt.

FOR MORE INFORMATION

To speak to an information specialist, call (202) 707-3000 (TTY: (202) 707-6737), Monday through Friday, 8:30 a.m. to 5:00 p.m., eastern time, excluding federal holidays. Recorded information is available 24 hours a day. Order forms and other publications from:
Library of Congress
Copyright Office
Publications Section, LM-455
101 Independence Avenue, S.E.
Washington, D.C. 20559-6000
or call the Forms and Publications Hotline 24 hours a day at (202) 707-9100. Most circulars (but not forms) are available via fax. Call (202) 707-2600 from a touchtone phone and follow the prompts. Access and download circulars, forms, and other information from the Copyright Office Website at www.copyright.gov.

Library of Congress · Copyright Office · 101 Independence Avenue, S.E. · Washington, D.C. 20559-6000
www.copyright.gov

August 2003—xxxx Web Rev: August 2003 ♻ Printed on recycled paper

U.S. Government Printing Office: 2003-xxx

Index

About the Author

Traci Truly received her law degree and undergraduate business degree from Baylor University. She has practiced law in Dallas, Texas since 1985, and has represented many small businesses. She currently represents Omni Entertainment, a Dallas entertainment company, and Mustang Booking Agency, also located in Dallas. Ms. Truly has written or coauthored several legal guides, including *How to Start a Business in Texas* and *Teen Rights (and Responsibilities)*, which was named to the New York Public Library's 2003 Books for Teen Age list. She has appeared on Fox Television (The Rob Nelson Show) and on the Fox New Channel (Dayside with Linda Vestor) and in *Seventeen Magazine*.

SPHINX® PUBLISHING ORDER FORM

TO:		SHIP TO:	

	Terms	F.O.B.	Chicago, IL	Ship Date

Charge my: ☐ VISA ☐ MasterCard ☐ American Express   ☐ **Money Order or Personal Check**

Credit Card Number   Expiration Date

Qty	ISBN	Title	Retail	Qty	ISBN	Title	Retail
	SPHINX PUBLISHING NATIONAL TITLES				1-57248-345-8	How to Form Your Own Corporation (4E)	$26.95
	1-57248-363-6	101 Complaint Letters That Get Results	$18.95		1-57248-232-X	How to Make Your Own Simple Will (3E)	$18.95
	1-57248-361-X	The 529 College Savings Plan (2E)	$18.95		1-57248-479-9	How to Parent with Your Ex	$12.95
	1-57248-483-7	The 529 College Savings Plan Made Simple	$7.95		1-57248-379-2	How to Register Your Own Copyright (5E)	$24.95
	1-57248-460-8	The Alternative Minimum Tax	$14.95		1-57248-394-6	How to Write Your Own Living Will (4E)	$18.95
	1-57248-349-0	The Antique and Art Collector's Legal Guide	$24.95		1-57248-156-0	How to Write Your Own	$24.95
	1-57248-347-4	Attorney Responsibilities & Client Rights	$19.95			Premarital Agreement (3E)	
	1-57248-382-2	Child Support	$18.95		1-57248-504-3	HR for Small Business	$14.95
	1-57248-487-X	Cómo Comprar su Primera Casa	$8.95		1-57248-230-3	Incorporate in Delaware from Any State	$26.95
	1-57248-148-X	Cómo Hacer su Propio Testamento	$16.95		1-57248-158-7	Incorporate in Nevada from Any State	$24.95
	1-57248-462-4	Cómo Negociar su Crédito	$8.95		1-57248-474-8	Inmigración a los EE.UU. Paso a Paso (2E)	$24.95
	1-57248-463-2	Cómo Organizar un Presupuesto	$8.95		1-57248-400-4	Inmigración y Ciudadanía en los EE. UU.	$16.95
	1-57248-147-1	Cómo Solicitar su Propio Divorcio	$24.95			Preguntas y Respuestas	
	1-57248-373-3	The Complete Adoption and Fertility Legal Guide	$24.95		1-57248-377-6	The Law (In Plain English)® for Small Business	$19.95
	1-57248-166-8	The Complete Book of Corporate Forms	$24.95		1-57248-476-4	The Law (In Plain English)® for Small Writers	$16.95
	1-57248-383-0	The Complete Book of Insurance	$18.95		1-57248-453-5	Law 101	$16.95
	1-57248-499-3	The Complete Book of Personal Legal Forms	$24.95		1-57248-374-1	Law School 101	$16.95
	1-57248-500-0	The Complete Credit Repair Kit	$19..95		1-57248-223-0	Legal Research Made Easy (3E)	$21.95
	1-57248-458-6	The Complete Hiring and Firing Handbook	$19.95		1-57248-449-7	The Living Trust Kit	$21.95
	1-57248-353-9	The Complete Kit to Selling Your Own Home	$18.95		1-57248-165-X	Living Trusts and Other Ways to	$24.95
	1-57248-229-X	The Complete Legal Guide to Senior Care	$21.95			Avoid Probate (3E)	
	1-57248-498-5	The Complete Limited Liability Company Kit	$21.95		1-57248-486-1	Making Music Your Business	$18.95
	1-57248-391-1	The Complete Partnership Book	$24.95		1-57248-186-2	Manual de Beneficios para el Seguro Social	$18.95
	1-57248-201-X	The Complete Patent Book	$26.95		1-57248-220-6	Mastering the MBE	$16.95
	1-57248-369-5	Credit Smart	$18.95		1-57248-455-1	Minding Her Own Business, 4E	$14.95
	1-57248-163-3	Crime Victim's Guide to Justice (2E)	$21.95		1-57248-480-2	The Mortgage Answer Book	$14.95
	1-57248-251-6	The Entrepreneur's Internet Handbook	$21.95		1-57248-167-6	Most Val. Business Legal Forms	$21.95
	1-57248-235-4	The Entrepreneur's Legal Guide	$26.95			You'll Ever Need (3E)	
	1-57248-346-6	Essential Guide to Real Estate Contracts (2E)	$18.95		1-57248-388-1	The Power of Attorney Handbook (5E)	$22.95
	1-57248-160-9	Essential Guide to Real Estate Leases	$18.95		1-57248-332-6	Profit from Intellectual Property	$28.95
	1-57248-375-X	Fathers' Rights	$19.95		1-57248-329-6	Protect Your Patent	$24.95
	1-57248-450-0	Financing Your Small Business	$17.95		1-57248-376-8	Nursing Homes and Assisted Living Facilities	$19.95
	1-57248-459-4	Fired, Laid-Off or Forced Out	$14.95		1-57248-385-7	Quick Cash	$14.95
	1-57248-502-7	The Frequent Traveler's Guide	$14.95		1-57248-350-4	El Seguro Social Preguntas y Respuestas	$16.95
	1-57248-331-8	Gay & Lesbian Rights	$26.95		1-57248-386-5	Seniors' Rights	$19.95
	1-57248-139-0	Grandparents' Rights (3E)	$24.95		1-57248-217-6	Sexual Harassment: Your Guide to Legal Action	$18.95
	1-57248-475-6	Guía de Inmigración a Estados Unidos (4E)	$24.95		1-57248-378-4	Sisters-in-Law	$16.95
	1-57248-187-0	Guía de Justicia para Víctimas del Crimen	$21.95		1-57248-219-2	The Small Business Owner's Guide to Bankruptcy	$21.95
	1-57248-253-2	Guía Esencial para los Contratos de	$22.95		1-57248-395-4	The Social Security Benefits Handbook (4E)	$18.95
		Arrendamiento de Bienes Raices			1-57248-216-8	Social Security Q&A	$12.95
	1-57248-334-2	Homeowner's Rights	$19.95		1-57248-328-8	Starting Out or Starting Over	$14.95
	1-57248-164-1	How to Buy a Condominium or Townhome (2E)	$19.95		1-57248-525-6	Teen Rights (and Responsibilities) (2E)	$14.95
	1-57248-384-9	How to Buy a Franchise	$19.95		1-57248-457-8	Tax Power for the Self-Employed	$17.95
	1-57248-497-7	How to Buy Your First Home (2E)	$14.95		1-57248-366-0	Tax Smarts for Small Business	$21.95
	1-57248-472-1	How to File Your Own Bankruptcy (6E)	$21.95		1-57248-236-2	Unmarried Parents' Rights (2E)	$19.95
	1-57248-343-1	How to File Your Own Divorce (5E)	$26.95		1-57248-362-8	U.S. Immigration and Citizenship Q&A	$18.95
	1-57248-390-3	How to Form a Nonprofit Corporation (3E)	$24.95		**Form Continued on Following Page**	**SubTotal**	

Qty	ISBN	Title	Retail
	1-57248-387-3	U.S. Immigration Step by Step (2E)	$24.95
	1-57248-392-X	U.S.A. Immigration Guide (5E)	$26.95
	1-57248-478-0	¡Visas! ¡Visas! ¡Visas!	$9.95
	1-57248-477-2	The Weekend Landlord	$16.95
	1-57248-451-9	What to Do—Before "I DO"	$14.95
	1-57248-330-X	The Wills, Estate Planning and Trusts Legal Kit	$26.95
	1-57248-473-X	Winning Your Personal Injury Claim (3E)	$24.95
	1-57248-225-7	Win Your Unemployment Compensation Claim (2E)	$21.95
	1-57248-333-4	Working with Your Homeowners Association	$19.95
	1-57248-380-6	Your Right to Child Custody, Visitation and Support (3E)	$24.95
	1-57248-505-1	Your Rights at Work	$14.95

CALIFORNIA TITLES

Qty	ISBN	Title	Retail
	1-57248-489-6	How to File for Divorce in CA (5E)	$26.95

Qty	ISBN	Title	Retail
	1-57248-356-3	How to Form a C...	
	1-57248-490-X	How to Form a L...	
	1-57071-401-0	How to Form a P...	
	1-57248-456-X	How to Make a ...	
	1-57248-354-7	How to Probate and Settle an Estate in FL (5E)	$26.95
	1-57248-339-3	How to Start a Business in FL (7E)	$21.95
	1-57248-204-4	How to Win in Small Claims Court in FL (7E)	$18.95
	1-57248-381-4	Land Trusts in Florida (7E)	$29.95
	1-57248-338-5	Landlords' Rights and Duties in FL (9E)	$22.95

GEORGIA TITLES

Qty	ISBN	Title	Retail
	1-57248-340-7	How to File for Divorce in GA (5E)	$21.95
	1-57248-493-4	How to Start a Business in GA (4E)	$21.95

ILLINOIS TITLES

Qty	ISBN	Title	Retail
	1-57248-244-3	Child Custody, Visitation, and Support in IL	$24.95
	1-57248-206-0	How to File for Divorce in IL (3E)	$24.95
	1-57248-170-6	How to Make an IL Will (3E)	$16.95
	1-57248-265-9	How to Start a Business in IL (4E)	$21.95
	1-57248-252-4	Landlord's Legal Guide in IL	$24.95

MARYLAND, VIRGINIA AND THE DISTRICT OF COLUMBIA

Qty	ISBN	Title	Retail
	1-57248-240-0	How to File for Divorce in MD, VA, and DC	$28.95
	1-57248-359-8	How to Start a Business in MD, VA, or DC	$21.95

MASSACHUSETTS TITLES

Qty	ISBN	Title	Retail
	1-57248-115-3	How to Form a Corporation in MA	$24.95
	1-57248-466-7	How to Start a Business in MA (4E)	$21.95
	1-57248-398-9	Landlords' Legal Guide in MA (2E)	$24.95

MICHIGAN TITLES

Qty	ISBN	Title	Retail
	1-57248-467-5	How to File for Divorce in MI (4E)	$24.95
	1-57248-182-X	How to Make a MI Will (3E)	$16.95
	1-57248-468-3	How to Start a Business in MI (4E)	$21.95

MINNESOTA TITLES

Qty	ISBN	Title	Retail
	1-57248-142-0	How to File for Divorce in MN	$21.95
	1-57248-179-X	How to Form a Corporation in MN	$24.95
	1-57248-178-1	How to Make a MN Will (2E)	$16.95

NEW JERSEY TITLES

Qty	ISBN	Title	Retail
	1-57248-239-7	How to File for Divorce in NJ	$24.95
	1-57248-448-9	How to Start a Business in NJ	$21.95

NEW YORK TITLES

Qty	ISBN	Title	Retail
	1-57248-193-5	Child Custody, Visitation and Support in NY	$26.95
	1-57248-351-2	File for Divorce in NY	$26.95
	1-57248-249-4	How to Form a Corporation in NY (2E)	$24.95
	1-57248-401-2	How to Make a NY Will (3E)	$16.95
	1-57248-468-1	How to Start a Business in NY (3E)	$21.95
	1-57248-198-6	How to Win in Small Claims Court in NY (2E)	$18.95
	1-57248-197-8	Landlords' Legal Guide in NY	$24.95
	1-57248-122-6	Tenants' Rights in NY	$21.95

NORTH CAROLINA AND SOUTH CAROLINA TITLES

Qty	ISBN	Title	Retail
		...le for Divorce in NC (3E)	$22.95
		...ake a NC Will (3E)	$16.95
		...tart a Business in NC or SC	$24.95
		...Rights & Duties in NC	$21.95

OHIO TITLES

Qty	ISBN	Title	Retail
		...le for Divorce in OH (3E)	$24.95
	1-57248-174-9	How to Form a Corporation in OH	$24.95
	1-57248-173-0	How to Make an OH Will	$16.95

PENNSYLVANIA TITLES

Qty	ISBN	Title	Retail
	1-57248-242-7	Child Custody, Visitation and Support in PA	$26.95
	1-57248-495-0	How to File for Divorce in PA (4E)	$26.95
	1-57248-358-X	How to Form a Corporation in PA	$24.95
	1-57248-094-7	How to Make a PA Will (2E)	$16.95
	1-57248-357-1	How to Start a Business in PA (3E)	$21.95
	1-57248-245-1	Landlords' Legal Guide in PA	$24.95

TEXAS TITLES

Qty	ISBN	Title	Retail
	1-57248-171-4	Child Custody, Visitation, and Support in TX	$22.95
	1-57248-399-7	How to File for Divorce in TX (4E)	$24.95
	1-57248-470-5	How to Form a Corporation in TX (3E)	$24.95
	1-57248-255-9	How to Make a TX Will (3E)	$16.95
	1-57248-496-9	How to Probate and Settle an Estate in TX (4E)	$26.95
	1-57248-471-3	How to Start a Business in TX (4E)	$21.95
	1-57248-111-0	How to Win in Small Claims Court in TX (2E)	$16.95
	1-57248-355-5	Landlords' Legal Guide in TX	$24.95

SubTotal This page _____
SubTotal previous page _____
Shipping— $5.00 for 1st book, $1.00 each additional _____
Illinois residents add 6.75% sales tax _____
Connecticut residents add 6.00% sales tax _____

Total _____

DISCARD